Nature In Verse

mary i. lovejoy

Nabu Public Domain Reprints:

You are holding a reproduction of an original work published before 1923 that is in the public domain in the United States of America, and possibly other countries. You may freely copy and distribute this work as no entity (individual or corporate) has a copyright on the body of the work. This book may contain prior copyright references, and library stamps (as most of these works were scanned from library copies). These have been scanned and retained as part of the historical artifact.

This book may have occasional imperfections such as missing or blurred pages, poor pictures, errant marks, etc. that were either part of the original artifact, or were introduced by the scanning process. We believe this work is culturally important, and despite the imperfections, have elected to bring it back into print as part of our continuing commitment to the preservation of printed works worldwide. We appreciate your understanding of the imperfections in the preservation process, and hope you enjoy this valuable book.

NATURE IN VERSE

A POETRY READER FOR CHILDREN

COMPILED BY

MARY I. LOVEJOY

SILVER, BURDETT & COMPANY

NEW YORK   BOSTON   CHICAGO

1897

CHOICE READING FOR SCHOOLS.

The Normal Course in Reading.
By Miss EMMA J. TODD, Formerly Training Teacher in Aurora, Ill., Public Schools, and W. B. POWELL, A.M., Supt. Schools, Washington, D.C.

A complete system of Reading, comprising six readers, three alternate readers, and Primary Reading Charts.

The Rational Method in Reading.
By EDWARD G. WARD, Associate Supt. Public Instruction, Brooklyn, N.Y.

Sight and phonetic reading combined: Readers, Manual of Instruction, and Phonetic Cards.

The Young Folks' Library.
Edited by LARKIN DUNTON, LL.D., Head Master Boston Normal School.

STORIES OF CHILD LIFE: four volumes.
THE WORLD AND ITS PEOPLE: eight volumes (including two in preparation).

Twilight Stories.
By ELIZABETH E. FOULKE.

A collection of charming original stories and poems, fully illustrated, for lower primary grades.

COPYRIGHT, 1895,
BY SILVER, BURDETT & COMPANY.

Harvard College Library
Jan. 21, 1910
from

Norwood Press
J. S. Cushing & Co. — Berwick & Smith
Norwood Mass. U.S.A.

TO MY NIECE

𝕸𝖆𝖗𝖌𝖆𝖗𝖊𝖙

Speak to the children, Little Book,
   And bring to them happy hours;
Teach them to find in every verse
   God's message in the flowers,
His loving care of beast and bird,
   His wonders in the deep,
His patience in His perfect work,
   His care o'er all who sleep;
And learn from all His teachings true
   How much a little child can do.

M. I. L.

PREFACE.

THE object of nature study is twofold: first, to arouse and cultivate the habit of observation; and, second, to impress the facts thus acquired upon the mind and the memory. What more delightful medium than verse for transmitting the beauties of nature to the awakened perceptions of childhood?

Children are natural lovers of poetry; its musical rhythm pleases the ear, its charm of expression stimulates the imagination, and they are easily led to search for the deeper beauty of meaning.

The need of a nature-poetry reader for the lower school grades has long been felt, and it was to meet this obvious want that the present volume has been compiled. It is intended to cover the first four years of school work, and the selections have been carefully graded with a view to adapting them to the varying ages and needs of those who will use the book. A division has been made into Songs of Spring, Summer, Autumn, and Winter, and under each head will be found a wide range of selections, from the simple rhymes suited to the younger readers, to more elaborate poems such as older pupils can easily read and comprehend.

The scheme of nature study, as outlined in the school work of the year, has been carefully followed. Plants, flowers, insects, birds, clouds and wind, rain and snow, and other phenomena, form the subject of diverse poems by different authors, and the teacher will find no difficulty in selecting such as are best suited to her grade, and to the lesson in hand.

Though primarily intended for school use, it is believed that the volume will prove no less attractive for children in the home. The poems are largely by the best English and American authors, and will bear frequent reading; while the memorizing of them will afford lasting pleasure and profit to their young readers.

The copyrighted material is used by permission of and by arrangement with Messrs. Houghton, Mifflin and Co., Roberts Bros., D. Appleton and Co., Harper and Bros., The Century Co., Lothrop Publishing Co., Charles Scribner's Sons, Kindergarten Publishing Co., Educational Publishing Co., and the publishers of the *Youth's Companion, Independent, New England Magazine*, and *Ladies' Home Journal*, to all of whom the compiler desires to make cordial acknowledgment for their courtesy and good will. Her thanks are also gratefully extended to the authors who so graciously granted permission for the use of their poems, and whose kindly letters have been a source of gratification and encouragement. That the book into which so much good thought has been incorporated may awaken in children a true love of the beautiful in nature, and a reverence for its Creator, is the earnest desire of the compiler.

TABLE OF CONTENTS.

SONGS OF SPRING.

		PAGE
The King of Glory	Holy Bible	3
The Coming of Spring	Selected	4
Spring Song	Selected	4
A Spring Song	*Children's Friend and Kindergarten*	5
A Walk in Spring	M. A. Stoddart	6
A Spring Meeting	*Harper's Young People*	7
A Song of Spring	Helen C. Bacon	8
The Sunshine's Caress	*Songs and Games for Little Ones*	9
Sunbeams	Selected	10
The Sunbeams	Emilie Poulsson	10
If I were a Sunbeam	Lucy Larcom	11
Spring Harbingers	Selected	12
The Seed	Selected	14
Wingèd Seeds	Helen Gray Cone	15
Nature's Thoughtfulness	M. F. Butts	15
Work	Selected	16
How the Wind Blows	Selected	17
Merry Rain	Selected	18
April Shower	Selected	20
Who Likes the Rain?	Clara Doty Bates	20
Stop, Stop, Pretty Water	Mrs. Follen	21
The Voice of the Grass	Mary Howitt	22
The Grass	Emily Dickinson	23
The Crocus's Soliloquy	Miss H. F. Gould	24
The Venturesome Buds	A. C.	25
The Tree	Björnstjerne Björnson	26
The Tree	Jones Very	27
The Weather-cock's Complaint	Selected	28

TABLE OF CONTENTS.

		PAGE
The Leaflets	Kate L. Brown	29
If ever I See	Lydia Maria Child	30
Little Rain-drops	*Aunt Effie's Rhymes*	31
Rain	Margaret Deland	31
The Little Lazy Cloud	Selected	32
Forest Trees	*Mother Truth's Melodies*	33
Hide-and-Seek	Frank Dempster Sherman	35
A Laughing Chorus	Selected	36
The Snowdrop	*Songs for the Little Ones at Home*	37
The First Snowdrop	Julia M. Dana	38
In April	Emily Gail Arnold	39
The Pussy Willow	Selected	40
Pussy Willow	Selected	41
Miss Willow	Susie E. Kennedy	42
The Polliwog	Selected	43
Jack in the Pulpit	*Whittier's Child Life*	44
Suppose	Selected	47
The Arbutus	Selected	48
Wishing	W. Allingham	49
April Fools	Emily Huntington Miller	50
The Mayflowers	J. G. Whittier	51
The Flower Bed	Selected	52
May	Helen B. Curtis	53
Apple Blossoms	Selected	54
May	R. M. Alden	54
The Violet	Barry Cornwall	55
Flower Dances	From the German, Mrs. Anderson	56
The Violet	Jane Taylor	58
Our Garden	Juliana Horatia Ewing	58
Seven times Four	Jean Ingelow	60
Field Flowers	Selected	61
Almost Time	Selected	62
Wake up, Little Daisy	Selected	63
The Daisy	Selected	64
The Daisy	James Montgomery	65
Dandelion	Kate L. Brown	66
Dandelion	Nellie M. Garabrant	67
Seven times One	Jean Ingelow	68
The Lilac	Clara Doty Bates	69
The Chicken's Mistake	Phœbe Cary	70
Rover in Church	Selected	71

TABLE OF CONTENTS.

		PAGE
Planted Himself to Grow	Selected	73
Bird Trades	Selected	73
The Little Doves	Selected	74
Changelings	M. F. Butts	75
Ragged Robin	L. A. Twamley	76
The Song of the Storm	James Buckham	77
The Ground Laurel	Miss H. F. Gould	78
A Bird's Nest	Florence Percy	79
Brother Robin	Mrs. Anderson	80
The Chimney Nest	Mary Barker Dodge	81
The Robin	Celia Thaxter	82
Don't Kill the Birds	J. Colesworthy	83
Anxiety	George Macdonald	84
Robert of Lincoln	William Cullen Bryant	86
Marjorie's Almanac	Thomas Bailey Aldrich	89
The Monkey	Mary Howitt	90
The Pigeon House	*Blades and Flowers*	92
Now the Sun is Sinking	Selected	92
Lullaby	E. Cavazza	93
Twinkle, Twinkle, Little Star	Jane Taylor	94
The Stars are Coming	Selected	95
God's Father-care	After the German, C. M. Harris	96

SONGS OF SUMMER.

Psalm XXIII	HOLY BIBLE	99
The Works of God	Jane Taylor	99
The Use of Flowers	Mary Howitt	100
We Thank Thee	Selected	102
A Song of Summer	Selected	102
Merry Sunshine	Selected	104
Summer Time	Selected	104
The Sunbeam	Selected	105
Little Sunbeam	Laura E. Richards	107
The Four Sunbeams	M. K. B.	109
Little Nannie	Lucy Larcom	111
A Summer Day	Selected	112
Music of Nature	Selected	113
Under the Greenwood Tree	William Shakespeare	114
Summer Woods	Mary Howitt	115

TABLE OF CONTENTS.

		PAGE
In the Meadow	Selected	115
The River	Samuel G. Goodrich	116
The Clouds	Selected	117
The Dew	Selected	118
Rain in Summer	W. C. Bennett	119
Summer Shower	Emily Dickinson	120
A Song of Clover	"Saxe Holm"	121
Pebbles	Frank Dempster Sherman	122
What the Burdock was Good for	Selected	122
Lily's Ball	*Fun and Earnest*	124
Pansy Song	Selected	125
The Lily of the Valley	Percival	126
A Child to a Rose	*Poems for a Child*	127
Forget-me-not	Selected	128
Discontent	Susan Coolidge	128
Great-Grandmother's Garden	M. J. Jacques	130
The Poppy	Jane Taylor	131
Chorus of the Flowers	Lucy Wheelock	131
Fashions at the Court of Queen Flora	Lydia Hoyt Farmer	133
Who Was She?	Selected	135
The Butterfly	Selected	137
The Butterfly's Lesson	Selected	137
The Grasshopper	*The Independent*	139
The Song of the Bee	Marian Douglass	140
The Busy Bee	Isaac Watts	141
The Mocking-bird's Song	J. R. Drake	142
Suppose	Alice Cary	144
Out-of-door Arithmetic	Selected	144
Letting the Old Cat Die	Selected	145
The Spider and the Fly	Mary Howitt	147
O Lark of the Summer Morning	From the Japanese	150
The Peacock	*Songs for the Little Ones at Home*	150
Nursery Song	Mrs. Carter	151
In the Swing	Eudora S. Bumstead	153
Good-night and Good-morning	Lord Houghton	154
The Bank-swallows	Selected	155
Three o'Clock in the Morning	R. S. Palfrey	157
Who Stole the Bird's Nest?	Lydia Maria Child	158
The Peter-bird	Henry Thompson Stanton	160
A Fable	*Popular Educator*	162
The Birds' Lawn Party	*Child Garden*	163

		PAGE
The Happy Bird	Selected	166
The Hidden Songster	Selected	166
Truant	S. A. Hudson	167
Ladybird, Ladybird	Caroline B. Southey	168
Ladybug, Ladybug	Selected	169
Mrs. Brindle's Cowslip Feast	Selected	170
The Oxen	Selected	172
Mrs. Pussy	Selected	173
A Boy's Song	"The Ettrick Shepherd"	174
The Cotton Plant	Selected	175
Two of a Trade	S. W. Duffield	176
A Summer Lullaby	E. S. Bumstead	177
The Song in the Night	James Buckham	178
Japanese Lullaby	Eugene Field	179
Cradle Song	Caris Brooke	180
Childhood Fancies	*Mother Truth's Melodies*	181

SONGS OF AUTUMN.

The Seasons	Helen Adelaide Ricker	187
Lost: The Summer	R. M. Alden	188
Autumn	Albert Laighton	189
Autumn Song	E. C. Stedman	189
About the Fairies	Selected	190
Trifles	Colesworthy	191
Sunshine	Selected	192
September	Helen Hunt Jackson	193
Goldenrod	Mrs. F. J. Lovejoy	193
Goldenrod	Selected	194
In September	*Sunday Afternoon*	196
The Spirit of the Sunset	Selected	197
Gentian	Kate L. Brown	197
Marigolds	Susan Hartley	198
The Flax Flower	Mary Howitt	199
The Wind	*Mother Truth's Melodies*	201
The Points of the Compass	Selected	202
Autumn Leaves	Selected	203
The Little Leaves	George Cooper	204
How the Leaves Come down	Susan Coolidge	205
October's Bright Blue Weather	Helen Hunt Jackson	206
October's Party	*Song Stories for Little Folks*	208

TABLE OF CONTENTS.

		PAGE
Little by Little	Selected	209
A Chance	Selected	210
The Chestnut Burr	Selected	210
Nutting	Selected	211
Little Nut People	E. J. Nicholson	212
The Gossip of the Nuts	Selected	214
The Squirrel's Arithmetic	Selected	215
Time Enough	Selected	216
Plant Song	Nellie M. Brown	217
Hither, Meadow Gossip, Tell Me!	H. Prescott Beach	218
Maude and the Cricket	Selected	219
The Cricket	William Cowper	221
The Frog's Good-bye	Selected	221
The Shining Web	Selected	222
The Wandering of the Birds	*Songs for the Little Ones at Home*	223
The Sparrow's Nest	Mary Howitt	225
The Wild Rabbits	Selected	226
Corn	Selected	227
A Lesson	Selected	228
The Child and the World	Selected	229
A National Flower	Lucy Larcom	231
Two Wise Owls	Selected	232
Tom	Constance Fenimore Woolson	233
The Rainy Day	Henry Wadsworth Longfellow	235
November	Alice Cary	235
Thanksgiving Day	Lydia Maria Child	236
The Raccoon	*Mother Truth's Melodies*	238
The Ant an Engineer	Selected	239
The Day is Done	Henry Wadsworth Longfellow	240
The Setting Sun	Selected	242
At Sunset	Mattie A. W. Clark	243
Twinkle, Twinkle	*Mother Truth's Melodies*	244
The New Moon	Mrs. Follen	245
A Naughty Little Comet	Ella Wheeler Wilcox	246
Norse Lullaby	Eugene Field	247
Ho, for Slumberland!	Eben C. Rexford	248
Can you Count the Stars?	Selected	249

SONGS OF WINTER.

		PAGE
Morning Hymn	Selected	253
Bird with Bosom Red	Selected	254
The Four Winds	Frank Dempster Sherman	255
What the Winds Bring	E. C. Stedman	255
The Fog	*Mother Truth's Melodies*	256
The Rain	*Mother Truth's Melodies*	257
The Little Artist	Selected	257
Jack Frost	Selected	258
Frost Pictures	Selected	259
The Frost	Miss H. F. Gould	261
Little Snowflakes	M. M.	262
Help One Another	Selected	263
Little Snowflakes	Selected	264
The First Snow	Selected	264
The Snow-shower	Mary Lundie Duncan	265
Little Ships in the Air	E. A. Rand	266
The Snow-shower	W. C. Bryant	267
The Snow-storm	Selected	269
The Disappointed Snowflakes	Selected	270
It Snows! It Snows	*Mother Truth's Melodies*	270
Snow	A. E. C.	271
The Snow-bird	Selected	272
The Snow-bird's Song	F. C. Woodward	273
Waiting to Grow	Selected	274
Come Here, Little Robin	*Easy Poetry*	275
What the Snow-birds Said	Selected	276
Our Sir Robin	Selected	278
The Christmas Silence	Margaret Deland	278
Merry Christmas	Selected	279
Holly	Susan Hartley	280
Said Tulip, "That Is So,"	Madge Elliot	282
Winter Apples	Hattie Whitney	283
Dance of the Months	Selected	284
* The Little Pine Tree	From the German, Eudora S. Bumstead	285
Pine Needles	Selected	288
Three Trees	Selected	288
The Body	Selected	290
Two and One	Selected	291
What the Coal Says	Selected	292

The Canary's Story	E. V. S.	292
The Little Kittens	Selected	294
They Didn't Think	Phœbe Cary	295
The Beautiful Island of Ceylon	Phillips Brooks	297
The Ferry for Shadowtown	*Motherhood*	298
The Star's Ball	*Ladies' Home Journal*	299
Our Flag	Selected	300
Hurrah for the Flag	Selected	301
Sweet and Low	Tennyson	302
Dutch Lullaby	Eugene Field	303
Good-night	Sydney Dayre	304
Now the Day is over	Sabine Baring-Gould	305

SONGS OF SPRING.

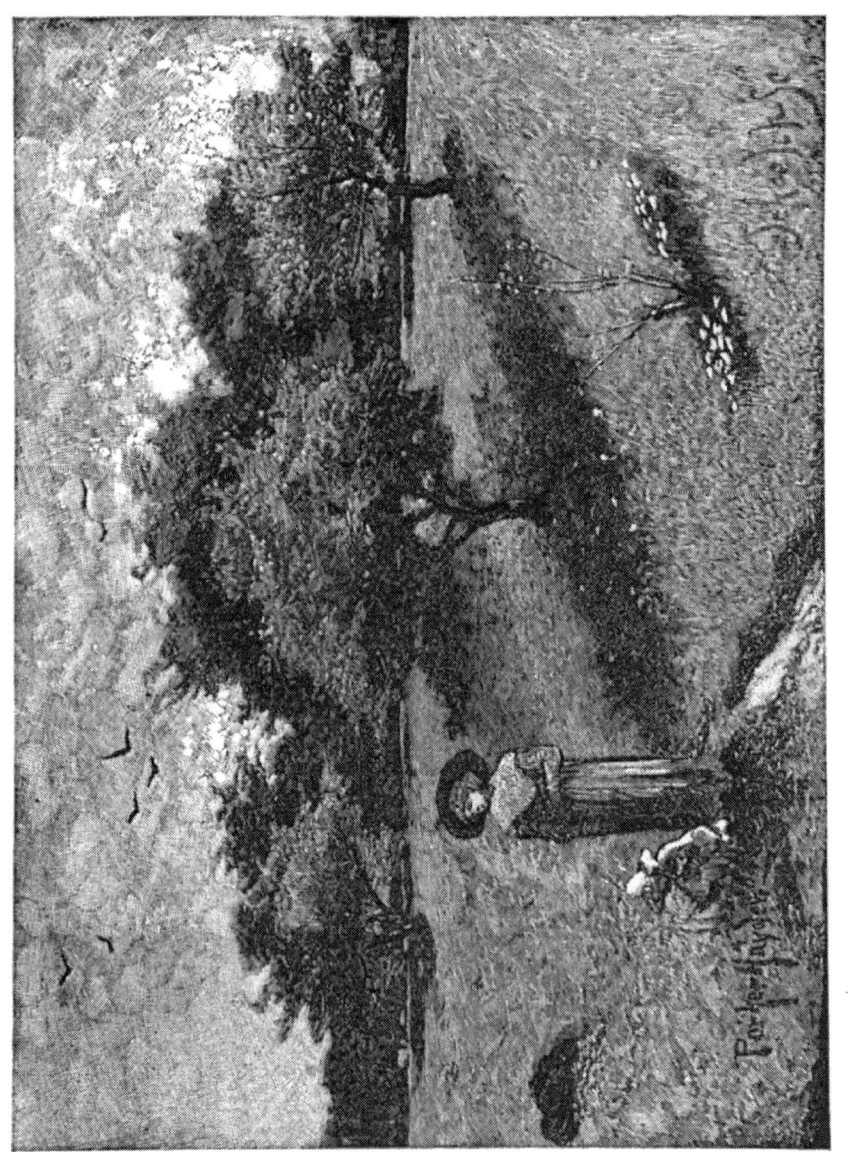

"I like to see the daisy and the buttercups once more,
The primrose and the cowslips, too, and every pretty flower."

Songs of Spring.

THE KING OF GLORY.

THE earth is the Lord's, and the fullness thereof,
The world and they that dwell therein;
For he hath founded it upon the seas,
And established it upon the floods.

Who shall ascend into the hill of the Lord?
Or who shall stand in his holy place?

He that hath clean hands, and a pure heart,
Who hath not lifted up his soul unto vanity,
He shall receive the blessing from the Lord,
And righteousness from the God of his salvation.

Lift up your heads, O ye gates!
And be ye lifted up, ye everlasting doors!
And the King of Glory shall come in.

Who is this King of Glory?

The Lord strong and mighty;
The Lord mighty in battle.

THE COMING OF SPRING.

THE birds are coming home soon;
    I look for them every day;
I listen to catch the first wild strain,
    For they must be singing by May.

The bluebird, he'll come first, you know,
    Like a violet that has taken wings;
And the red-breast trills while his nest he builds,
    I can hum the song that he sings.

And the crocus and wind-flower are coming, too;
    They're already upon the way;
When the sun warms the brown earth through and through,
    I shall look for them *any* day.

Then be patient, and wait a little, my dear;
    "They're coming," the winds repeat;
"We're coming! we're coming!" I'm sure I hear,
    From the grass blades that grow at my feet.

                          — *Selected.*

SPRING SONG.

"AWAKE," said the sunshine; "'tis time to get up;
    Awake, pretty daisy and sweet buttercup.
Why! you've been sleeping the whole winter long;
Hark! hark! don't you hear? 'Tis the bluebird's first
    song."

"Awake," call the streamlets. "We've lain here so still,
And now we must all go to work with a will."
"Wake," says the warm breeze, "and you, willow tree,
Come, put on your leaves in a twinkling for me!"

"Awake," breathes the air from the blue sky above,
"Awake, for the air is all beauty and love.
Wake, little children so merry and dear;
Ah! what were the spring, if you were not here!"
—*Selected.*

A SPRING SONG.

OLD Mother Earth woke up from her sleep,
    And found she was cold and bare;
The winter was over, the spring was near,
And she had not a dress to wear.
"Alas!" she sighed, with great dismay,
"Oh, where shall I get my clothes?
There's not a place to buy a suit,
And a dressmaker no one knows."

"I'll make you a dress," said the springing grass,
Just looking above the ground,
"A dress of green of the loveliest sheen,
To cover you all around."
"And we," said the dandelions gay,
"Will dot it with yellow bright."
"I'll make it a fringe," said forget-me-not,
"Of blue, very soft and light."

"We'll embroider the front," said the violets,
"With a lovely purple hue."

"And we," said the roses, "will make you a crown
Of red, jeweled over with dew."
"And we'll be your gems," said a voice from the shade,
Where the ladies' ear-drops live —
"Orange is the color for any queen
And the best we have to give."

Old Mother Earth was thankful and glad,
As she put on her dress so gay;
And that is the reason, my little ones,
She is looking so lovely to-day.
— *Children's Friend and Kindergarten.*

A WALK IN SPRING.

I'M very glad the spring is come: the sun shines out so bright,
The little birds upon the trees are singing for delight;
The young grass looks so fresh and green, the lambs do sport and play,
And I can skip and run about as merrily as they.

I like to see the daisy and the buttercups once more,
The primrose, and the cowslip too, and every pretty flower:
I like to see the butterfly extend her painted wing,
And all things seem, just like myself, so pleased to see the spring.

The fishes in the little brook are jumping up so high,
The lark is singing sweetly as she mounts unto the sky,

The rooks are building up their nests upon the great
    oak tree,
And everything's as busy and as happy as can be.

There's not a cloud upon the sky, there's nothing dark
    or sad;
I jump, and scarce know what to do, I feel so very
    glad.
God must be very good indeed, who made each pretty
    thing;
I'm sure we ought to love him much for bringing back
    the spring.
— *M. A. Stoddart.*

A SPRING MEETING.

(From Harper's Young People, by permission. Copyright, 1891, by Harper and Brothers.)

HULLO, Bob Wren!
    Are you back again?
Glad to see you so well and so merry;
Fear we're here rather early this year!
Dear, but I wish I'd a bite of a cherry!
Just ripe in the South,
Melt in your mouth.
Weren't you sorry to leave the sunny
Land of bloom, and of bees and honey?

By-and-by here 'twill be bright and jolly
With bud and blossom, but somehow now
The atmosphere seems melancholy,
For there's not a leaf on a single bough.

And the wind, oh, how it makes you shiver,
And long for the balmy air that blows
The reeds that quiver
Above some river
That warm in Floridian sunlight flows!

Have you any new songs to sing this season?
And do you know where you are going to stop?
We've taken rooms in the very top
Of "The Maple"— prices quite within reason.
You've a flat near by that you've leased till fall?
How nice! Then surely you'll come and call.

A SONG OF SPRING.

I HEARD the bluebird singing
　To robin in the tree.
"Cold winter now is over
And spring has come," said he;
"'Tis time for flowers to rouse from sleep,
And from their downy blankets peep;
So wake, wake, little flowers,
Wake, for winter is o'er,
Wake, wake, wake,
The spring has come once more."

Said robin to the bluebird,
"My nest I now must build,
And shortly you shall see it
With pretty blue eggs filled.

Then let us join once more and sing;
So wake, wake, little flowers,
That all the flowers may know 'tis spring;
Wake, for winter is o'er,
Wake, wake, wake,
The spring has come once more."

The robin and the bluebird
Soon after flew away,
But as they left the tree-top,
I think I heard them say,
"If birds and flowers have work to do,
Why, so have little children too;
So work, work, little children,
Work, for winter is o'er,
Work, work, work,
The spring has come once more."
— *Helen C. Bacon.*

THE SUNSHINE'S CARESS.

TO the little brown cradles,
  Where the leaf babies sleep,
Came the sunshine with a soft caress,
And whispered, " Buds, dear little buds,
Throw off your old winter wraps,
And put on your new spring dress;"
So said the sunshine with its soft caress.

From the cradles they peeped
With a timid gaze;
Just to answer this soft caress,

They quickly courtesied a sweet "Good-day";
Then donned they all new dresses so gay;
And they said, "The world we'll bless;
Thank you, Sunshine, for your soft caress."
— *Miss Jenk's Songs and Games for Little Ones.*

SUNBEAMS.

MERRY little sunbeams,
    Flitting here and there;
Joyous little sunbeams,
Dancing everywhere.
Come they with the morning light,
And chase away the gloomy night.

Kind words are like sunbeams,
That sparkle as they fall;
And loving smiles are sunbeams,
  A light of joy to all.
In sorrow's eye they dry the tear,
And bring the fainting heart good cheer.
— *Selected.*

THE SUNBEAMS.

"NOW, what shall I send to the Earth to-day?"
    Said the great, round, golden Sun.
"Oh! let us go down there to work and play,"
  Said the Sunbeams, every one.

So down to the Earth in a shining crowd,
  Went the merry, busy crew;
They painted with splendor each floating cloud
  And the sky while passing through.

"Shine on, little Star, if you like," they cried;
  "We will weave a golden screen
That soon all your twinkling and light shall hide,
  Though the Moon may peep between."

The Sunbeams then in through the windows crept,
  To the children in their beds —
They poked at the eyelids of those who slept,
  Gilded all the little heads.

"Wake up, little children!" they cried in glee,
  "And from Dreamland come away!
We've brought you a present: wake up and see!
  We have brought you a sunny day!"
— *Emilie Poulsson.*

IF I WERE A SUNBEAM.

"IF I were a sunbeam,
  I know what I'd do:
I would seek white lilies
  Rainy woodlands through:
I would steal among them,
  Softest light I'd shed,
Until every lily
  Raised its drooping head.

NATURE IN VERSE.

"If I were a sunbeam,
  I know where I'd go:
Into lowliest hovels,
  Dark with want and woe:
Till sad hearts looked upward,
  I would shine and shine;
Then they'd think of heaven,
  Their sweet home and mine."

Art thou not a sunbeam,
  Child whose life is glad
With an inner radiance
  Sunshine never had?
Oh, as God has blessed thee,
  Scatter rays divine!
For there is no sunbeam
  But must die, or shine.
    — *Lucy Larcom.*

SPRING HARBINGERS.

OUR Mother Earth is in her loom,
  A-weaving night and day;
Her new spring carpet must be done
  Before the month of May!

Just see the stripes of red, and green,
  Of yellow, brown, and blue!
In warp and woof I've never seen
  A web of such rare hue.

Our grand snow king is melting down,
    And never more will rise;
The icicles that spike his crown
    Have dwindled, too, in size;

And busy fingers I behold,
    That weave with fairy floss,
As on the bare rocks, hard and cold,
    They spread their mats across.

My heart leaps high, as, far and wide,
    Where'er I chance to stray,
I find sweet harbingers that hide
    Their elfin forms away,

Down deep within the tangled woods,
    With that bright swarm of bees,
The birds, the butterflies, the buds,
    That seek such haunts as these.

Weave on, weave on, dear Mother Earth,
    Thy carpet warm and bright,
Of warp and woof thou hast no dearth;
    And oh, with what delight

We'll make its folds spread o'er the land
    In length and breadth complete;
And praise the kind and loving hand
    That placed it 'neath our feet.

—*Selected.*

NATURE IN VERSE.

THE SEED.

AS wonderful things are hidden away
   In the heart of a little brown seed,
As ever were found in the fairy net
   Of which children sometimes read.

Over its pretty shining coat
   We sprinkle the earth so brown,
And the sunshine warms its lowly bed,
   And the rain comes dropping down.

Patter, patter, the soft, warm rain
   Knocks at the tiny door,
And two little heads come peeping out,
   Like a story in fairy lore.

One is the Caulicle creeping down,
   At the first but a wee white root;
The other the Plumule; above the soil
   It sends up a little green shoot.

Steadily up toils the slender stem,
   And only its work it heeds;
A leaf appears, buds, blossoms, and fruit,
   Last of all come the little seeds.

Then its work all done, if an annual,
   It has had its brief, bright day,
And now at the touch of the Frost-king's breath
   It withers and fades away.
                            — *Selected.*

WINGED SEEDS.

OH, gold-green wings, and bronze-green wings,
    And rose-tinged wings, that down the breeze
Come sailing from the maple trees!
You showering things, you shimmering things,
That June-time always brings!
Oh, are you seeds that seek the earth,
The shade of lovely leaves to spread?
Or shining angels, that had birth
When kindly words were said?

Oh, downy dandelion wings,
Wild-floating wings like silver spun,
That dance and glisten in the sun!
You airy things, you elfin things,
That June-time always brings!
Oh, are you seeds that seek the earth,
The light of laughing flowers to spread?
Or flitting fairies, that had birth
When merry words were said?
                —*Helen Gray Cone—St. Nicholas.*

NATURE'S THOUGHTFULNESS.

SO busy is the dear old earth,
    A-weaving million tresses
And making for her forest-trees
The freshest of new dresses;
A-spreading carpets o'er the dales
Embroidered with sweet posies,
A-molding petals velvet soft,
And making up her roses:

So busy is the dear old earth
Her spreading meadows over,
A-storing honey in the cells
Of her vast fields of clover:
A-carving scarlet lily cups,
A setting blue-bells ringing,
And teaching all her baby birds
The newest rules of singing;
So busy is the dear old earth
Through every summer morning:—
Pray tell me why this eager haste,
This marvelous adorning,
The fringed petals, tinted cups,
The wondrous variation?—
Methinks she's getting ready for
Her boys' and girls' vacation.
— *M. F. Butts.*

WORK.

DOWN and up, and up and down,
   Over and over and over;
Turn in the little seed, dry and brown,
   Turn out the bright red clover.
Work, and the sun your work will share,
   And the rain in its time will fall;
For Nature, she worketh everywhere,
   And the grace of God through all.

With hand on the spade and heart in the sky,
   Dress the ground and till it;

Turn in the little seed, brown and dry,
   Turn out the golden millet.
Work, and your house shall be duly fed;
   Work, and rest shall be won;
I hold that a man had better be dead
   Than alive, when his work is done!

Down and up, and up and down,
   On the hill-top, low in the valley;
Turn in the little seed, dry and brown,
   Turn out the rose and lily.
Work, with a plan, or without a plan,
   And your ends shall be shaped true;
Work, and learn at first-hand, like a man —
   The best way to know is to do!

Down and up till life shall close,
   Ceasing not your praises;
Turn in the wild, white winter snows,
   Turn out the sweet spring daisies.
Work, and the sun your work will share,
   And the rain in its time will fall;
For Nature, she worketh everywhere,
   And the grace of God through all.

—Selected.

HOW THE WIND BLOWS!

HIGH and low
   The spring winds blow!
They take the kites that the boys have made,
   And carry them off high into the air;

They snatch the little girls' hats away,
   And toss and tangle their flowing hair.

    High and low
   The summer winds blow!
They dance and play with the garden flowers,
   And bend the grasses and yellow grain;
They rock the bird in her hanging nest,
   And dash the rain on the window-pane.

    High and low
   The autumn winds blow!
They frighten the bees and blossoms away,
   And whirl the dry leaves over the ground;
They shake the branches of all the trees,
   And scatter ripe nuts and apples around.

    High and low
   The winter winds blow!
They fill the hollows with drifts of snow,
   And sweep on the hills a pathway clear;
They hurry the children along to school,
   And whistle a song for the happy New Year.
                           —*Selected.*

MERRY RAIN.

SPRINKLE, sprinkle, comes the rain,
   Tapping on the window-pane!
   Trickling, coursing,
   Crowding, forcing,
     Tiny rills
   To the dripping window-sills.

SONGS OF SPRING.

Laughing rain-drops, light and swift,
Through the air they fall and sift;
    Dancing, tripping,
    Bounding, skipping,
        Through the street,
With their thousand merry feet.

Every blade of grass around
Is a ladder to the ground;
    Clinging, striding,
    Slipping, sliding,
        On they come
    With their busy, patt'ring hum.

In the woods, by twig and spray,
To the roots they find their way;
    Rushing, creeping,
    Doubling, leaping,
        Down they go
    To the waiting life below.

O the brisk and merry rain,
Bringing gladness in its train!
    Falling, glancing,
    Tinkling, dancing,
        All around —
    Listen to its cheery sound!

—Selected.

APRIL SHOWER.

PATTER, patter, let it pour,
    Patter, patter, let it roar;
Down the steep roof let it rush,
Down the hillside let it gush;
'Tis the welcome April shower,
Which will wake the sweet Mayflower.

Patter, patter, let it pour,
Patter, patter, let it roar;
Let the vivid lightning flash,
Let the headlong thunder dash,
'Tis the welcome April shower,
Which will wake the sweet Mayflower.

Patter, patter, let it pour,
Patter, patter, let it roar;
Soon the clouds will burst away,
Soon will shine the bright spring day,
Soon the welcome April shower
Will awake the sweet Mayflower.
—Selected.

WHO LIKES THE RAIN?

"I" SAID the duck, "I call it fun,
    For I have my little red rubbers on;
  They make a cunning three-toed track
In the soft, cool mud. Quack! Quack! Quack!"

"I," cried the dandelion, "I,
My roots are thirsty, my buds are dry;"
And she lifted a towsled yellow head
Out of her green and grassy bed.

"I hope 'twill pour! I hope 'twill pour!"
Purred the tree-toad at his gray back door,
"For, with a broad leaf for a roof,
I am perfectly weather proof."

Sang the brook: "I laugh at every drop,
And wish they never need to stop
Till a big, big river I grew to be,
And could find my way out to the sea."

"I," shouted Ted, "for I can run,
With my high-top boots and my rain-coat on,
Through every puddle and runlet and pool
That I find on my way to school."
—*Clara Doty Bates.*

STOP, STOP, PRETTY WATER.

"STOP, stop, pretty water!"
  Said Mary one day,
To a frolicsome brook
That was running away.

"You run on so fast!
I wish you would stay:
My boat and my flowers
You will carry away.

"But I will run after;
Mother says that I may;
For I would know where
You are running away."

So Mary ran on;
But I have heard say,
That she never could find
Where the brook ran away.
— *Mrs. Follen.*

THE VOICE OF THE GRASS.

HERE I come creeping, creeping everywhere;
    By the dusty roadside,
    On the sunny hillside,
    Close by the noisy brook,
    In every shady nook,
I come creeping, creeping everywhere.

Here I come creeping, creeping everywhere;
    All around the open door,
    Where sit the aged poor,
    Here where the children play,
    In the bright, merry May,
I come creeping, creeping everywhere.

Here I come creeping, creeping everywhere;
    In the noisy city street,
    My pleasant face you'll meet
    Cheering the sick at heart,
    Toiling his busy part,
Silently creeping, creeping everywhere.

Here I come creeping, creeping everywhere;
    You cannot see me coming,
    You hear my low, sweet humming;
    For in the starry night,
    And the glad morning light,
I come, quietly creeping everywhere.

* * * * * * * *

Here I come creeping, creeping everywhere;
    When you're numbered with the dead
    In your still and narrow bed,
    In the happy spring I'll come,
    And deck your silent home,
Creeping silently, creeping everywhere.

— Mary Howitt.

THE GRASS.

The grass has so little to do, —
    A spear of simple green,
With only butterflies to brood,
And bees to entertain,

And stir all day to pretty tunes
The breezes fetch along,
And hold the sunshine in its lap,
And bow to everything;

And thread the dews all night, like pearls,
And make itself so fine, —
A duchess were too common
For such a noticing.

And even when it dies, to pass
In odors so divine, —
As lowly spices gone to sleep,
Or amulets of pine.

And then to dwell in sovereign barns,
And dream the days away, —
The grass so little has to do,
I wish I were the hay!
— *Emily Dickinson.*

THE CROCUS'S SOLILOQUY.

DOWN in my solitude under the snow,
  Where nothing cheering can reach me —
Here, without light to see how to grow,
  I'll trust to Nature to teach me.

I will not despair, nor be idle, nor frown,
  Locked in so gloomy a dwelling;
My leaves shall run up, and my roots shall run down,
  While the bud in my bosom is swelling.

Soon as the frost will get out of my bed,
  From this cold dungeon to free me,
I will peep up with my little bright head,
  And all will be joyful to see me.

Then from my heart will young petals diverge,
  As rays of the sun from their focus;
I from the darkness of earth will emerge,
  A happy and beautiful crocus.

Gayly arrayed in my yellow and green,
  When to their view I have risen,
Will they not wonder how one so serene
  Came from so dismal a prison?

Many, perhaps, from so simple a flower,
  This little lesson may borrow,—
Patient to-day, through its gloomiest hour,
  We come out the brighter to-morrow.
          —*Miss H. F. Gould.*

THE VENTURESOME BUDS.

LAST autumn, when winter was taking
  His last cosy nap in his bed,
And each little leaf bud was sleeping,
  With blankets pulled over its head,

We crept half-way out of our cradles;
  The sun kissed us sadly; the air
Was colder, by far, than we liked it;
  The pines whispered softly—"Beware!"

But just then old Winter came roaring
  And rushing down over the hill:—
At the first awful blast of the trumpet
  Our poor little hearts stood still.

He clutched us so with cold fingers
  We nearly were choking to death;
And rustled us so with his breezes
  We came near to losing our breath.

And then growing tenderer towards us,
   He made us white hoods, warm and nice,
And fastened them under our noses
   With quaint little buckles of ice.

But, an hour ago, a dear bluebird
   Perched here on our trembling spray,
And sang, and sang, and sang, and sang,
   Till he sang old Winter away.

Now we must each meet the springtime
   With a frost-bitten nose or an ear.
We shall sleep like all the sensible buds
   When Winter comes round next year.

—*A. C.*

THE TREE.

THE Tree's early leaf-buds were bursting their brown:
   "Shall I take them away?" said the Frost, sweeping down.
      "No, let them alone
      Till the blossoms have grown,"
Prayed the Tree, while it trembled from rootlet to crown.

The Tree bore its blossoms and all the birds sung:
"Shall I take them away?" said the Wind, as it swung.
      "No, let them alone
      Till the berries have grown,"
Said the Tree, while its leaflets, quivering, hung.

The Tree bore its fruit in the midsummer glow:
Said the girl, "May I gather thy sweet berries now?"
    "Yes, all thou canst see:
    Take them; all are for thee,"
Said the Tree, while it bent down its laden boughs low.
              — *Björnstjerne Björnson.*

THE TREE.

I LOVE thee when thy swelling buds appear,
   And one by one their tender leaves unfold,
As if they knew that warmer suns were near,
Nor longer sought to hide from winter's cold;
And when with darker growth thy leaves are seen
To veil from view the early robin's nest,
I love to lie beneath thy waving screen,
With limbs by summer's heat and toil oppressed;
And when the autumn winds have stripped thee bare,
And round thee lies the smooth, untrodden snow,
When naught is thine that made thee once so fair,
I love to watch thy shadowy form below,
And through thy leafless arms to look above
On stars that brighter beam when most we need their love
              — *Jones Very.*

THE WEATHER-COCK'S COMPLAINT.

NO wonder he creaks as the winds go by,
No wonder he turns with a misty sigh;
How would you like a living earning
By turning — turning — turning — turning?
Or to stand all your life with a pole for a base
And the winds of all weathers to blow in your face?

"Creak, creak, creak," we hear him say,
"To-morrow will be like yesterday,—
Now to the east, now to the west —
One never has any quiet or rest;
An hour of sunshine, another of rain,
It's nothing but turning and turning again."

"Creak, creak, creak," the tin bird cries,
"In quite a few signs the secret lies;
When the wind's from the west, there's nothing to fear;
When the wind's from the east, a storm is near:
Can't every one tell when the day is clear
Without keeping me turning and twisting here?"

"Creak, creak, creak," the weather-cock growls,
"I think I'm the most ill used of fowls;
I never foretold bad weather yet
But you went in while I got wet;
Say what you may, I don't think it's right
To keep me twisting from morning to night."

— Selected.

THE LEAFLETS.

DANCE, little leaflets, dance,
'Neath the tender sky of Spring;
Dance in the golden sun,
To the tune that the robins sing.
Now you are light and young,
Just fit for a baby play;
So dance, little leaflets, dance,
And welcome the merry May.

Sway, little leaflets, sway,
In the ardent sunlight's glow;
Oh, what a sleepy world!
For August has come, you know.
Many a drowsy bird
Is drooping its golden crest,
So sway, little leaves, and rock
The orioles in their nests.

Swing, little leaflets, swing;
The quail pipes in the corn;
Under the harvest sun,
The cardinal flow'r is born.
Russet and gold and red,
Little leaves are gayly dress'd;
Is it holiday time with you
That you have put on your best?

Fall, little leaflets, fall,
Your mission is not sped;
Shrill pipes the Winter wind,
And the happy Summer's dead.

Make now a blanket warm,
For the leaves till the Spring-winds call;
You must carpet the waiting earth,
So fall, little leaflets, fall.
— *Kate L. Brown.*

IF EVER I SEE.

IF ever I see,
  On bush or tree,
Young birds in their pretty nest,
  I must not, in play,
  Steal the birds away,
To grieve their mother's breast.

  My mother, I know,
  Would sorrow so,
Should I be stolen away;
  So I'll speak to the birds
  In my softest words
Nor hurt them in my play.

  And when they can fly
  In the bright blue sky,
They'll warble a song to me;
  And then if I'm sad
  It will make me glad
To think they are happy and free.
—*Lydia Maria Child.*

LITTLE RAIN-DROPS.

OH, where do you come from,
  You little drops of rain,
Pitter-patter, pitter-patter,
Down the window-pane?
They say I'm very naughty,
But I've nothing else to do,
But sit here at the window;
I should like to play with you.

Tell me, little rain-drops,
Is that the way you play,
Pitter-patter, pitter-patter,
All the rainy day?
The little rain-drops cannot speak,
But "pitter-patter, pat"
Means, "We can play on this side;
Why can't you play on that?"

—*Selected.*

RAIN.

"Rain, rain, go away,
  Come again another day!"

OH, the dancing leaves are merry,
  And the bloss'ming grass is glad,
But the river's too rough for the ferry
  And the sky is low and sad.

Yet the daisies shake with laughter
  As the surly wind goes by,

For they know what is hurrying after,
  As they watch the dim, gray sky;

The clovers are rosy with saying —
  (The buttercups bend to hear)
"Oh, be patient, it is only delaying —
  Be glad, for it's very near."

The blushing pimpernel closes;
  It isn't because it grieves —
And down in the garden, the roses
  Smile out from their lattice of leaves!

Such gladness has stirred the flowers!
  Yet children only complain:
"Oh, what is the use of showers?"
"Oh, why does it ever rain?"
— Margaret Deland.

THE LITTLE LAZY CLOUD.

A PRETTY little cloud away up in the sky,
  Said it did not care if the earth was dry:
'Twas having such a nice time sailing all around,
It wouldn't, no, it wouldn't, tumble on the ground.

So the pretty little lilies hung their aching heads,
And the golden pansies cuddled in their beds;
The cherries couldn't grow a bit, you would have pitied them;
They'd hardly strength to hold to the little slender stem.

By and by the little cloud felt a dreadful shock,
Just as does a boat when it hits upon a rock;
Something ran all through it, burning like a flame,
And the little cloud began to cry as down to earth it came.

Then old Grandpa Thunder, as he growled away,
Said, "I thought I'd make you mind 'fore another day:
Little clouds were meant to fall when the earth is dry,
And not go sailing round away up in the sky."

And old Grandma Lightning, flitting to and fro,
Said, "What were you made for, I would like to know,
That you spend your precious time sailing all around,
When you know you ought to be buried in the ground?"

Then lilies dear and pansies all began to bloom,
And the cherries grew and grew till they took up all the
    room.
Then by and by the little cloud, with all its duty done,
Was caught up by a rainbow and allowed a little fun.
—Selected.

FOREST TREES.

CHILDREN, have you seen the budding
    Of the trees in valleys low?
Have you watched it creeping, creeping
    Up the mountain, soft and slow?
        Weaving there a plush-like mantle,
    Brownish, grayish, reddish green,
Changing, changing, daily, hourly,
    Till it smiles in emerald sheen?

Have you watched the shades so varied,
　　From the graceful, little white birch,
Faint and tender, to the balsam's
　　Evergreen, so dark and rich?
Have you seen the quaint mosaics
　　Gracing all the mountain-sides,
Where they, mingling, intertwining,
　　Sway like softest mid-air tides?

Have you seen the autumn frostings
　　Spread in all the leafage bright, —
Frostings of the rarest color,
　　Red and yellow, dark and light?
Have you seen the glory painted
　　On the mountain, valley, hill,
When the landscape, all illumined,
　　Blazons forth His taste and skill?

Have you seen the foliage, dropping,
　　Tender cling, as loth to leave
Mother-trees that taught them deftly
　　All their warp and woof to weave?
Have you seen the leafless branches
　　Tossing wildly 'gainst the blue?
Have you seen the soft gray beauty
　　Of their wintry garments' hue?

Have you thought the resurrection
　　Seen in Nature year by year
Is a symbol of our rising
　　In a higher, holier sphere?
Children, ye are buds maturing;
　　Make your autumn rich and grand,
That your winter be a passage
　　Through the gates to Glory-land.
　　　　　　　　—*Mother Truth's Melodies.*

HIDE-AND-SEEK.

NOW hide the flowers beneath the snow,
   And Winter shall not find them;
Their safety nooks he cannot know;
   They left no tracks behind them.

The little brooks keep very still,
   Safe in their ice-homes lying;
Let Winter seek them where he will,
   There's no chance for his spying.

Gone are the birds; they're hiding where
   The Winter never searches;
Safe in the balmy Southern air,
   They sing on sunlit perches.

But comes the Spring at last to look
   For all her playmates hidden,
And one by one — flower, bird, and brook —
   Shall from its place be bidden.

Then shall the world be glad and gay,
   The birds begin their chorus,
The brooks sing, too, along their way,
   And flowers spring up before us!

Frank Dempster Sherman.

A LAUGHING CHORUS.

OH, such a commotion under the ground
  When March called, "Ho, there! ho!"
Such spreading of rootlets far and wide,
  Such whispering to and fro;
And, "Are you ready?" the Snowdrop asked,
  "'Tis time to start, you know."
"Almost, my dear," the Scilla replied;
  "I'll follow as soon as you go."
Then, "Ha! ha! ha!" a chorus came
  Of laughter soft and low,
From the millions of flowers under the ground —
  Yes — millions — beginning to grow.

"I'll promise my blossoms," the Crocus said,
  "When I hear the bluebirds sing."
And straight thereafter, Narcissus cried,
  "My silver and gold I'll bring."
"And ere they are dulled," another spoke,
  "The Hyacinth bells shall ring."
And the Violet only murmured, "I'm here,"
  And sweet grew the air of spring.
Then, "Ha! ha! ha!" a chorus came
  Of laughter soft and low,
From the millions of flowers under the ground —
  Yes — millions — beginning to grow.

Oh, the pretty, brave things! through the coldest days,
  Imprisoned in walls of brown,
They never lost heart though the blast shrieked loud,
  And the sleet and the hail came down,

But patiently each wrought her beautiful dress,
  Or fashioned her beautiful crown;
And now they are coming to brighten the world,
  Still shadowed by Winter's frown;
And well may they cheerily laugh, "Ha! ha!"
  In a chorus soft and low,
The millions of flowers hid under the ground —
  Yes — millions — beginning to grow.
                    — *Selected.*

THE SNOWDROP.

NOW the spring is coming on,
  Now the snow and ice are gone,
Come, my little snowdrop root,
Will you not begin to shoot?

Ah, I see your little head
Peeping from the flower-bed;
Looking out so green and gay,
On this fine and pleasant day.

For the mild south wind doth blow,
And hath melted all the snow;
And the sun shines out so warm,
You need not fear another storm.

So your pretty flowers show,
And your petals white undo;
Then you'll hang your modest head
Down upon my flower-bed.
                — *Songs for the Little Ones at Home.*

THE FIRST SNOWDROP.

"I WANT to get up," the Snowdrop said,
  As she loosened the wraps about her head.
"It may be the world is white with snow,
Yet I'd rather be there than here below.
'Tis horrid to be curled up so tight —
I want to look out and see the light.

"My dear little sisters are fast asleep,
And I am the first to take a peep
Out of my bed, where, snugly rolled,
I slept in warm blankets, fold on fold.
But now I am ever so wide awake,
And it's surely time for the morn to break.

"My dress is the prettiest e'er was seen;
'Tis white, with an overskirt of green,
With six pretty silken cords that hold
As many tiny tassels of gold.
Oh, I have been working, never fear,
To look my best, when I do appear.

"And I must welcome the song-birds home,
There seems such a stirring all around,
And I hear new voices above the ground.
The buds on the willows are calling, 'Come';
For this is the message they bring, I guess,
'Get up, little maid; it is time to dress.'"

—Julia M. Dana.

IN APRIL.

THE air is soft and balmy,
   The grass is growing green,
The maple buds are swelling,
   Till their slender threads are seen.
The brown brook chatters gayly
   Its rippling course along,
And hark! — from distant tree-top
   I hear the bluebird's song.

O joyous, gladsome carol,
   Exultant, fearless, true!
There is hidden a heavenly message
   'Neath that coat of heavenly blue.
My heart thrills as I listen;
   God's love is sure and strong.
Thank Him for life's awakening!
   Praise for the bluebird's song!

After the winter, springtime,
   The sunshine follows rain;
Tho' grief and sorrow chill us,
   The heart grows warm again.
From earth to His glad heaven
   God will His loved ones bring;
Still, after frosts and snowdrifts,
   We hear the bluebirds sing.

                   — *Emily Gail Arnold.*

THE PUSSY WILLOW.

DAINTY pussy willows
   On a swaying bough
Sang awhile to springtime,
   Soft and low.
What we heard them telling
   In the splashing rain
We will tell to you again.

"Yes, we are pussies,
   Though we never purr;
See, we are dressed
   In softest fur.
Children reach to gather us
   With loving care
As we gently sway in air.

"Come the gentle bluebirds
   When the warm winds blow.
Do we ever catch them?
   Oh, no! no!
We are no such pussies —
   Sad would be the spring
Did the dear birds never sing.

"By and by the rain came
   Knocking at the door;
Sunbeams coaxed us
   Sleep no more!
Out we sprang delighted;
   Now we gayly sing,
Through the merry hours of spring."
—Selected.

PUSSY WILLOW.

THE brook is brimmed with melting snow,
  The maple sap is running,
And on the highest elm a crow
  His coal-black wings is sunning.
A close, green bud, the Mayflower lies
  Upon its mossy pillow;
And sweet and low the south wind blows,
And through the brown fields calling goes,
  "Come, Pussy! Pussy Willow!
Within your close, brown wrapper stir;
Come out and show your silver fur;
  Come, Pussy! Pussy Willow!"

Soon red will bud the maple trees,
  The bluebirds will be singing,
And yellow tassels in the breeze
  Be from the poplars swinging;
And rosy will the Mayflower lie
  Upon its mossy pillow;
"But you must come the first of all, —
Come, Pussy!" is the south wind's call, —
  "Come, Pussy! Pussy Willow!
A fairy gift to children dear,
The downy firstling of the year, —
  Come, Pussy! Pussy Willow!"

— Selected.

MISS WILLOW.

A LADY so fine came out of the woods,
 All dressed in silvery gray,
Whether satin or velvet, or soft woolen goods,
 I'm sure I'm not able to say.

While great drifts were piled in hedgerow and plain,
 While fiercely the March winds did blow,
And wildly the tempest in mockery raged,
 This lady stepped out in the snow.

I asked a young ash which grew by the wall,
 To tell me the fine lady's name;
"Oh yes," he made answer, "no trouble at all;
 She has a most enviable fame.

"So modest is she, so dainty and sweet,
 Most dearly I love her, 'tis true,
But if no objection the young lady brings,
 I'll make her acquainted with you.

"Miss Willow, my friend, Mr. Love-Nature here,
 Your friendship has gallantly sought,"
Then, in a low whisper, he laughingly said,
 "We call her Miss Pussy for short."
                            —*Susie E. Kennedy.*

THE POLLIWOG.

A TINY little polliwog
  And little brothers three,
Lived in the water near a log,
  As happy as could be.

A-swimming, swimming all the day,
  A-sleeping all the night,
And trying, though they were so gay,
  To do just what was right.

A-growing, growing all the while,
  Because they did their best;
But I'm afraid that you will smile
  When I tell you the rest.

One morning, sitting on the log,
  They looked in mute surprise;
Four legs had every polliwog,
  Where two had met their eyes.

Their mother, letting fall a tear,
  Said, "Oh, my polliwogs,
It can't be you that're sitting here!"
  For all of them were frogs.

And with their legs they'd grown some lungs;
  So you just wait and see;
In summer time their little tongues
  Will sing "Ka-chink" with glee.

—Selected.

JACK IN THE PULPIT.

JACK in the pulpit
   Preaches to-day
Under the green trees
Just over the way.
Squirrel and song-sparrow
High on their perch
Hear the sweet lily-bells
Ringing to church.
Come, hear what his reverence
Rises to say,
In his low, painted pulpit
This calm Sabbath day.
Fair is the canopy
Over him seen,
Penciled by Nature's hand,
Black, brown and green.
Green is his surplice,
Green are his bands;
In his queer little pulpit
The little priest stands.
In black and gold velvet,
So gorgeous to see,
Comes with his bass voice
The chorister bee.
Green fingers playing
Unseen on wind-lyres —
Low singing bird voices —
These are his choirs.
The violets are deacons —
I know by the sign
That the cups which they carry

Are purple with wine;
And the columbines bravely
As sentinels stand
On the lookout with all their
Red trumpets in hand.
Meek-faced anemones,
Drooping and sad;
Great yellow violets,
Smiling out glad;
Buttercups' faces,
Beaming and bright;
Clovers, with bonnets —
Some red and some white;
Daisies, their white fingers
Half clasped in prayer;
Dandelions, proud of
The gold of their hair;
Innocents, — children,
Guileless and frail,
Meek little faces
Upturned and pale;
Wildwood geraniums,
All in their best,
Languidly leaning,
In purple gauze dressed; —
All are assembled
This sweet Sabbath day,
To hear what the priest
In his pulpit will say.
Look! white Indian pipes
On the green mosses lie!
Who has been smoking
Profanely so nigh?
Rebuked by the preacher,

NATURE IN VERSE.

The mischief is stopped;
But the sinners, in haste,
Have their little pipes dropped.
Let the wind, with the fragrance
Of fern and black birch,
Blow the smell of the smoking
Clean out of the church.
So much for the preacher;
The sermon comes next.
Shall we tell how he preached it
And what was his text?
Alas! like too many
Grown-up folks who play
At worship in churches
Man-builded to-day,
We heard not the preacher
Expound or discuss;
But we looked at the people,
And they looked at us.
We saw all their dresses,
Their colors and shapes,
The trim of their bonnets,
The cut of their capes.
We heard the wind-organ,
The bee and the bird,
But of Jack in the Pulpit
We heard not a word.

— *Whittier's Child Life.*

SUPPOSE.

SUPPOSE the little cowslip
Should hang its golden cup,
And say, "I'm such a tiny flower,
I'd better not grow up";
How many a weary traveler
Would miss its fragrant smell;
And many a little child would grieve
To lose it from the dell.

Suppose the little breezes,
Upon a summer's day,
Should think themselves too small
To cool the traveler on his way;
Who would not miss the smallest
And softest ones that blow,
And think they made a great mistake,
If they were talking so?

Suppose the little dewdrop
Upon the grass should say,
"What can a little dewdrop do?
I'd better roll away."
The blade on which it rested,
Before the day was done,
Without a drop to moisten it,
Would wither in the sun.

How many deeds of kindness
A little child can do,
Although it has but little strength
And little wisdom, too!

It wants a loving spirit,
Much more than strength, to prove
How many things a child may do
For others by its love.
—*Selected.*

THE ARBUTUS.

IT trailed on a sheltered hillside
  Where in summer grew woodland fern,
And the sunbeam's warm kisses fell on it,
Close nestled in coppice and herne!
The faded leaves covered it softly,
But when March passed over its bed,
It wakened affrighted to listen
And raised up its fair little head.
And when our dear April so gentle,
With its warm tears the little face kissed,
It spread out its green leaves above it,
And blushed very sweetly, I wist.
And when I had gone to the hillside
To welcome the springtime so new,
I was led by the delicate fragrance
To the place where the arbutus grew.
O timid and sweet little blossom!
A lesson thou bringest to me—
Though thy life it is fair in beholding,
It is hidden in humility.
—*Selected.*

WISHING.

RING-TING! I wish I were a primrose,
A bright yellow primrose blooming in the spring!
    The stooping boughs above me,
    The wandering bee to love me,
The fern and moss to creep across,
And the elm-tree for our king!

Nay — stay! I wish I were an elm-tree,
A great, lofty elm-tree with green leaves gay!
    The winds would set them dancing,
    The sun and moonshine glance in,
The birds would house among the boughs,
And ever sweetly sing!

O — no! I wish I were a robin,
A robin or a little wren, everywhere to go;
    Through forest, field, or garden,
    And ask no leave or pardon,
Till winter comes with icy thumbs
To ruffle up our wings!

Well — tell! Where should I fly to,
Where go to sleep in the dark wood or dell?
    Before a day was over,
    Home comes the rover,
For mother's kiss, — sweeter this
Than any other thing.

                                              — *W. Allingham.*

APRIL FOOLS.

SHY little pansies
   Tucked away to sleep,
Wrapped in brown blankets
Piled snug and deep,
Heard in a day-dream
A bird singing clear:
"Wake, little sweethearts;
The springtime is here!"

Glad little pansies,
Stirring from their sleep,
Shook their brown blankets
Off for a peep,
Put on their velvet hoods,
Purple and gold,
And stood all a-tremble
Abroad in the cold.

Snowflakes were flying,
Skies were grim and gray,
Bluebird and robin
Had scurried away;
Only the cruel wind
Laughed as it said,
"Poor little April fools,
Hurry back to bed!"

Soft chins a-quiver,
Dark eyes full of tears,
Brave little pansies,
Spite of their fears,

Said, "Let us wait for
The sunshiny weather;
Take hold of hands, dears,
And cuddle up together."
— *Emily H. Miller.*

THE MAYFLOWERS.

SAD Mayflower! watched by winter stars,
   And nursed by winter gales,
With petals of the sleeted spars,
   And leaves of frozen sails!

What had she in those dreary hours,
   Within her ice-rimmed bay,
In common with the wildwood flowers,
   The first sweet smiles of May?

Yet, "God be praised!" the Pilgrims said,
   Who saw the blossoms peer
Above the brown leaves, dry and dead;
   "Behold our Mayflower here!

"God wills it: here our rest shall be,
   Our years of wandering o'er,
For us the *Mayflower* of the sea
   Shall spread her sails no more."

O sacred flowers of faith and hope!
   As sweetly now as then
Ye bloom on many a birchen slope,
   In many a pine-dark glen.

Behind the sea-wall's rugged length,
   Unchanged, your leaves unfold,
Like love behind the manly strength
   Of the brave hearts of old.

So live the fathers in their sons:
   Their sturdy faith be ours
And ours the love that overruns
   Its rocky strength with flowers.

The Pilgrim's wild and wintry day
   Its shadow round us draws;
The Mayflower of his stormy bay,
   Our freedom's struggling cause.

But warmer suns erelong shall bring
   To life the frozen sod;
And, through dead leaves of hope, shall spring
   Afresh the flowers of God!

—*J. G. Whittier.*

THE FLOWER BED.

BABY, what do the blossoms say,
   Down in the garden walk?
They nod and bend in the twilight gray;
   Say! can you hear them talk?
They say, "Oh, darling baby bright,
We're going to sleep! good night, good night!
The gentle breezes have come to sing
How God takes care of everything."

Baby, what does the robin say,
  Do you hear his evening song?
He sits and sings his twilight lay,
  With a heart all merry and strong.
He sings, "Good night, my baby dear;
Sleep well, sleep soft, and do not fear;
For somehow I know as I sit and sing,
That God takes care of everything."

—Selected.

MAY.

STARTING, starting from the earth,
  See the pretty flowers!
Wakened from their winter's sleep
  By the springtime showers.

Now we know that May hath come,
  O'er the meadows dancing;
Robin lilts his sweetest song,
  Sunbeams round him glancing.

Bluebird 's knocking at the door,
  Swallow 's hither coming;
And, o'er all the sunny mead,
  Springtime bees are humming.

Golden sunshine, silver rain,
  Each its work is doing.
Birds and bees and blossoms fair,
  Now the world renewing.

O thou merry month o' May!
  We have come to meet you;
Little lads and lassies gay,
  Happily we greet you.

From your pretty flowers, dear,
  We will take a warning;
And we'll try our work to do
  In life's fair May morning.
—*Helen B. Curtis.*

APPLE BLOSSOMS.

THE orchard trees are white,
  For the bright May sun is shining,
    And the blossoms show
    Like a drift of snow,
From a cloud with a rosy lining.

And two little bright blue eyes,
With a sweet surprise are glowing;
  "Oh! mamma, I see
  A popcorn tree
And the corn-ball just a-growing."
—*Selected.*

MAY.

WHY are bees and butterflies
    Dancing in the sun?
Violets and buttercups
    Blooming, every one?

Why does Mr. Bobolink
  Seem so shocking gay?
Why does — ah! I'd half forgot!
  This is really May.

Why are all the water-bugs
  Donning roller-skates?
And the solemn lady-bugs
  Dozing on the gates?

Why do all the meadow brooks
  Try to run away,
As though some one were chasing them?
  Bless me! this is May.

Please to tell me why the trees
  Have put new bonnets on?
Please to tell me why the crows
  Their picnics have begun?

Why does all the whole big world
  Smell like a fresh bouquet
Picked from one of God's flower beds?
  Oh, I know! it's May.
          —*R. M. Alden — The Pansy.*

THE VIOLET.

I LOVE all things the seasons bring,
  All buds that start, all birds that sing,
  All leaves from white to jet,
All the sweet words that summer sends,
When she recalls her flowery friends,
  But chief — the Violet!

I love, how much I love the rose,
On whose soft lips the south wind blows,
　　In pretty amorous threat;
The lily paler than the moon,
The odorous, wondrous world of June,
　　Yet more — the Violet!

She comes, the first, the fairest thing
That Heaven upon the earth doth fling,
　　Ere Winter's star is set:
She dwells behind her leafy screen,
And gives, as angels give, unseen,
　　So, love — the Violet!

What modest thoughts the Violet teaches,
What gracious boons the Violet preaches,
　　Bright maiden, ne'er forget!
But learn, and love, and so depart,
And sing thou with thy wiser heart,
　　"Long live the Violet!"

—*Barry Cornwall.*

FLOWER DANCES.

IN May the valley lilies ring,
　　Their bells chime clear and sweet;
They cry, "Come forth, ye flowerets all,
　　And dance with twinkling feet."

The blossoms, gold and blue and white,
　　Come quickly, one and all;
The speedwell, the forget-me-not,
　　The violets hear the call.

Then in a trice the lilies play,
   While all to dance begin:
The moon looks on with friendly smile,
   And takes great joy therein.

Then sadly vexed is Master Frost,
   Down to the vale comes he;
Lilies play dancing tunes no more,
   The pretty blossoms flee.

Yet Frost has scarcely left the vale,
   When lilies far and near
Call quickly to the Springtide feast;
   Their bells ring doubly clear.

I'll stay no longer in the house;
   The lilies call me, too;
Sweet flowerets, dancing out-of-doors,
   I come to dance with you.

           —*From the German by Mrs. Anderson.*

THE VIOLET.

Down in a green and shady bed
   A modest violet grew;
Its stalk was bent, it hung its head,
   As if to hide from view.

And yet it was a lovely flower,
   Its color bright and fair;
It might have graced a rosy bower
   Instead of hiding there.

>   Yet there it was content to bloom,
>   In modest tints arrayed;
>   And there diffused its sweet perfume
>   Within the silent shade.
>
>   Then let me to the valley go,
>   This pretty flower to see,
>   That I may also learn to grow
>   In sweet humility.
>
> — *Jane Taylor.*

OUR GARDEN.

THE winter is gone, and at first Jack and I were sad,
  Because of the snow-man's melting, but now we are glad;
For the spring has come, and it's warm, and we're allowed
  to garden in the afternoon;
And summer is coming, and oh, how lovely our flowers
  will be in June!

We are so fond of flowers, it makes us quite happy to
  think
Of our beds — all colors — blue, white, yellow, purple,
  and pink,
Scarlet, lilac, and crimson! And we're fond of sweet
  scents as well,
And mean to have pinks, roses, sweet peas, mignonette,
  clove carnations, and everything good to smell.

On Monday we went to the wood and got primrose plants and a sucker of dog-rose;
It looks like a green stick in the midst of the bed at present, but wait till it blows!
The primroses were in full flower, and the rose ought to flower soon;
You've no idea how lovely it is in that wood in June!

The primroses look quite withered now I am sorry to say;
But that's not our fault, but nurse's, and it shows how hard it is to garden when you can't have your own way.
We planted them carefully and were just going to water them all in a lump,
When nurse fetched us both indoors, and put us to bed for wetting our pinafores at the pump.

We're going to take everything up, — for it can't hurt the plants to stand on the grass for a minute.
And you really can't make a bed smooth with so many things in it.
We shall dig it all over, and get leaf-mold from the wood, and hoe up the weeds;
And when it's tidy, we shall plant and put labels and strike cuttings and sow seeds.

We are so fond of flowers! Jack and I often dream at night
Of getting up and finding our garden ablaze with all colors, — blue, red, yellow, and white;
And midsummer's coming, and our big brother Tom will sit under the tree
With his book, and Mary will beg sweet nosegays of me.

It's so tiresome! Jack wants to build a greenhouse now.
He has found some bits of broken glass and an old window
    frame, and he says he knows how.
I tell him there's not glass enough, but he says there's lots.
And he's taken all the plants that belong to the bed and
    put them into pots.
— Juliana Horatia Ewing.

SEVEN TIMES FOUR.

HEIGH HO! daisies and buttercups,
    Fair yellow daffodils, stately and tall!
When the wind wakes how they rock in the grasses,
    And dance with the cuckoo-buds slender and small!
Here's two bonny boys, and here's mother's own lasses,
    Eager to gather them all.

Heigh ho! daisies and buttercups!
    Mother shall thread them a daisy chain;
Sing them a song of the pretty hedge-sparrow,
    That loved her brown little ones, loved them full fain;
Sing, "Heart, thou art wide though the house be but
    narrow"—
    Sing once, and sing it again.

Heigh ho! daisies and buttercups,
    Sweet wagging cowslips, they bend and they bow;
A ship sails afar over warm ocean waters,
    And haply one musing doth stand at her prow.
O bonny brown sons, and O sweet little daughters,
    Maybe he thinks on you now!

Heigh ho! daisies and buttercups,
  Fair yellow daffodils, stately and tall —
A sunshiny world full of laughter and leisure,
  And fresh hearts unconscious of sorrow and thrall!
Send down on their pleasure smiles passing its measure,
    God that is over us all!

— *Jean Ingelow.*

FIELD FLOWERS.

FIELD flowers, sweet field flowers,
  Fairies of the spring,
Only those who love them
  Know the joy they bring.
Love can but discover
  With their beauty, worth,
Jeweling all over
  All the bright green earth.
Field flowers, sweet field flowers,
  Fairies of the spring,
Only those who love them,
  Know the joy they bring.

Field flowers, sweet field flowers,
  Everywhere they come,
Whereso'er, unseeking,
  You may chance to roam.
With their smiles to meet us
  On each path of ours,

All unsought to greet us,
Come the sweet field flowers.
Field flowers, sweet field flowers,
Fairies of the spring,
Only those who love them,
Know the joy they bring.
— *Selected.*

ALMOST TIME.

Almost time for the pretty white daisies
  Out of their sleep to awaken at last,
And over the meadows, with grasses and clover,
  To bud and to blossom, and grow so fast;
Almost time for the buttercups yellow,
  The ferns and the flowers, the roses and all,
To waken from slumber, and merrily listen
  To gladden our hearts at the spring's first call.

Almost time for the skies to grow bluer,
  And breezes to soften, and days to grow long;
For eyes to grow brighter, and hearts to grow gladder
  And earth to rejoice in her jubilant song;
Almost time for the sweetest of seasons;
  Nearer it comes with each new-born day,
And soon the smile of the beautiful springtime
  Winter's cold shadow will chase away.
— *Selected.*

THE DAISY.

THE daisy is the meekest flower
   That grows in wood or field;
To wind and rain, and footsteps rude,
   Its slender stem will yield.

In spring it dots the green with white,
   And blossoms all the year,
And so it is a favorite flower,
   With all the children dear.

Before the stars are in the sky,
   The daisy goes to rest,
And folds its little shining leaves
   Upon its golden breast.

So children when they go to bed
   Should fold their hands in prayer,
And place themselves and all they love,
   In God's protecting care.
—*Selected.*

WAKE UP, LITTLE DAISY.

WAKE up, little Daisy, the summer is nigh,
　The dear little robin is up in the sky;
The snow-drop and crocus are never so slow,
Then, wake up, little Daisy, and hasten to grow.
Wake up, wake up, wake up, little Daisy,
And hasten to grow.

I tease pleasant sunshine to rest on your head,
The dew and the rain-drops to moisten your bed,
And then every morning I just take a peep,
To see your little face, but you're still fast asleep.
Wake up, wake up, wake up, little Daisy,
And hasten to grow.

Mother often tells me, if I would be wise,
And honored, and happy, I early must rise;
So I'm up in the morning, and out in the dew,
With all the little birds, and the honey-bees too.
Wake up, wake up, wake up, little Daisy,
And hasten to grow.

Listen, little Daisy, I'll tell you what's said,
The lark thinks you're lazy, and love your warm bed,
But I'll not believe it, for now I can see
Your bright little eyes softly winking at me.
Wake up, wake up, wake up, little Daisy,
And hasten to grow.

—*Selected.*

THE DAISY.

THERE is a flower, a little flower,
   With silver crest and golden eye,
That welcomes every changing hour,
   And weathers every sky.

It smiles upon the lap of May,
   To sultry August spreads its charm,
Lights pale October on his way,
   And twines December's arm.

'Tis Flora's page, in every place,
   In every season, fresh and fair;
It opens with perennial grace,
   And blossoms everywhere.

On waste and woodland, rock and plain,
   Its humble buds unheeded rise;
The Rose has but a summer reign:
   The Daisy never dies.

—*James Montgomery.*

DANDELION.

HE is a roguish little elf,
   A gay audacious fellow,
Who tramps about in doublet green
   And skirt of brightest yellow;
In ev'ry field, by ev'ry road,
   He peeps among the grasses,
And shows his sunny little face
   To ev'ry one that passes.

Within the churchyard he is seen,
   Beside the headstones peeping,
And shining like a golden star
   O'er some still form there sleeping;
Beside the house door oft he springs
   In all his wanton straying,
And children shout in laughing glee
   To find him in their playing.

At eve he dons his nightgown green,
   And goes to bed right early,
At morn, he spreads his yellow skirts
   To catch the dewdrops pearly;
A darling elf is Dandelion,
   A roguish wanton sweeting;
Yet he is loved by ev'ry child,
   All give him joyous greeting.

— *Kate L. Brown.*

DANDELION.

THERE'S a dandy little fellow,
   Who dresses all in yellow,
In yellow with an overcoat of green;
With his hair all crisp and curly,
In the springtime bright and early
A-tripping o'er the meadow he is seen.
Through all the bright June weather,
Like a jolly little tramp,
He wanders o'er the hillside, down the road;
Around his yellow feather,
The gypsy fireflies camp;
His companions are the wood lark and the toad.

But at last this little fellow
Doffs his dainty coat of yellow,
And very feebly totters o'er the green;
For he very old is growing
And with hair all white and flowing,
A-nodding in the sunlight he is seen.
Oh, poor dandy, once so spandy,
Golden dancer on the lea!
Older growing, white hair flowing,
Poor little baldhead dandy now is he!

                           —*Nellie M. Garabrant.*

SEVEN TIMES ONE.

THERE'S no dew left on the daisies and clover,
    There's no rain left in heaven;
I've said my "seven times" over and over,
    Seven times one are seven.

I am old, so old, I can write a letter;
    My birthday lessons are done;
The lambs play always, they know no better;
    They are only one times one.

O moon! in the night I have seen you sailing
    And shining so round and low;
You were bright! ah bright! but your light is failing—
    You are nothing now but a bow.

You moon, have you done something wrong in heaven
    That God has hidden your face?
I hope if you have you will soon be forgiven,
    And shine again in your place.

O velvet bee, you're a dusty fellow,
    You've powdered your legs with gold!
O brave marsh marybuds, rich and yellow,
    Give me your money to hold!

O columbine, open your folded wrapper
    Where two twin turtle-doves dwell!
O cuckoopint, toll me the purple clapper
    That hangs in your clear green bell!

And show me your nest with the young ones in it;
  I will not steal them away;
I am old! you may trust me, linnet, linnet —
  I am seven times one to-day.
—Jean Ingelow.

THE LILAC.

THE sun shone warm, and the lilac said,
  "I must hurry and get my table spread,
For if I am slow, and dinner late,
My friends, the bees, will have to wait."

So delicate lavender glass she brought
And the daintiest china ever bought,
Purple tinted, and all complete;
And she filled each cup with honey sweet.

"Dinner is ready!" the spring wind cried;
And from hive and hiding far and wide,
While the lilac laughed to see them come,
The little gray-jacketed bees came hum-m!

They sipped the sirup from every cell,
They nibbled at taffy and caramel;
Then, without being asked, they all buzzed, "We
Will be very happy to stay to tea."
—Clara Doty Bates.

THE CHICKEN'S MISTAKE.

A LITTLE downy chicken one day
   Asked leave to go on the water,
Where she saw a duck with her brood at play,
   Swimming and splashing about her.

Indeed, she began to peep and cry,
   When her mother wouldn't let her:
"If ducks can swim there, why can't I;
   Are they any bigger or better?"

Then the old hen answered, "Listen to me,
   And hush your foolish talking;
Just look at your feet and you will see
   They were only made for walking."

But chicky wistfully eyed the brook,
   And didn't half believe her,
For she seemed to say by a knowing look,
   "Such stories couldn't deceive her."

And as her mother was scratching the ground,
   She muttered lower and lower,
"I know I can go there and not get drowned,
   And so I think I'll show her."

Then she made a plunge where the stream was deep,
   And saw too late her blunder:
For she hadn't hardly time to peep
   Till her foolish head went under.

And now I hope her fate will show
   The child, my story reading,
That those who are older sometimes know
   What you will do well in heeding.

That each content in his place should dwell,
    And envy not his brother;
And any part that is acted well
    Is just as good as another.

For we all have our proper sphere below,
    And this is a truth worth knowing:
You will come to grief if you try to go
    Where you never were made for going.
                               —*Phœbe Cary.*

ROVER IN CHURCH.

'TWAS a Sunday morning in early May,
    A beautiful, sunny, quiet day,
And all the village, old and young,
Had trooped to church when the church bells rung;
The windows were open and breezes sweet
Fluttered the hymn books from seat to seat;
Even the birds in the pale-leaved birch
Sang as softly as if in church.

Right in the midst of the minister's prayer
There came a knock at the outer door.
"Who's there, I wonder!" the sexton thought
As his careful ear the tapping caught.
Rap — rap, rap — rap, — a louder sound —
The boy on the back seat turned around.
What could it mean? for never before
Had any tapped at the old church door.

Again the tapping, and now 'tis loud;
The minister paused — tho' his head was bowed.

Rap-pi-ty-rap! This will never do,
The girls are peeping and laughing too,
So the sexton tripped over the creaking floor,
Lifted the latch and opened the door;
In there trotted, as big as a bear,
A great black dog; with a solemn air,

Right up the center aisle he pattered —
People might laugh, it little mattered.
Straight he went to a little maid,
Who blushed and hid as though afraid,
And there sat down as if to say, —
" I'm sorry I was late to-day.
But better late than never, you know;
Beside I waited an hour or so,

"And couldn't get them to open the door,
Tho' I banged my tail, and knocked the floor.
Now, little mistress, I'm going to stay
And hear what the minister has to say."
The poor little girl hid her face and cried,
But the big dog nestled close to her side
And kissed her, dog fashion, tenderly,
Wondering what the matter could be!

The dog being large, and the sexton small,
He sat through the sermon and heard it all,
As solemn and wise as any one there,
With a very dignified scholarly air,
And, instead of scolding, the minister said,
As he laid his hand on the sweet child's head
After the service, " I never knew
Two better listeners than Rover and you."

—Selected.

PLANTED HIMSELF TO GROW.

DEAR, little, bright-eyed Willie,
   Always so full of glee,
Always so very mischievous,
   The pride of our home is he.

One bright summer day we found him
   Close by the garden wall,
Standing so grave and dignified
   Beside a sunflower tall.

His tiny feet he had covered
   With the moist and cooling sand;
The stalk of the great, tall sunflower
   He grasped with his chubby hand.

When he saw us standing near him,
   Gazing so wonderingly
At his babyship, he greeted us
   With a merry shout of glee.

We asked our darling what pleased him;
   He replied with a face aglow,
"Mamma, I'm going to be a man;
   I've planted myself to grow."
                          —Selected.

BIRD TRADES.

THE swallow is a mason,
   And underneath the eaves
He builds a nest, and plasters it
   With mud and hay and leaves.

Of all the weavers that I know,
    The oriole is the best;
High on the branches of the tree
    She hangs her cosy nest.

The woodpecker is hard at work —
    A carpenter is he —
And you may hear him hammering
    His nest high up a tree.

Some little birds are miners:
    Some build upon the ground:
And busy little tailors, too,
    Among the birds are found.
                                    — *Selected.*

THE LITTLE DOVES.

HIGH on the top of an old pine-tree
    Broods a mother-dove with her young ones three.
Warm over them is her soft, downy breast,
And they sing so sweetly in their nest.
"Coo," say the little ones, "Coo," says she,
All in their nest on the old pine-tree.

Soundly they sleep through the moonshiny night,
Each young one covered and tucked in tight;
Morn wakes them up with the first blush of light,
And they sing to each other with all their might.
"Coo," say the little ones, "Coo," says she,
All in their nest on the old pine-tree.

When in the nest they are all left alone,
While their mother far for their dinner has flown,

Quiet and gentle they all remain,
Till their mother they see come home again.
Then "Coo," say the little ones, "Coo," says she,
All in their nest on the old pine-tree.

When they are fed by their tender mother,
One never pushes nor crowds another;
Each opens wide his own little bill,
And he patiently waits, and gets his fill.
Then "Coo," say the little ones, "Coo," says she,
All in their nest on the old pine-tree.

Wisely the mother begins by and by,
To make her young ones learn to fly;
Just for a little way over the brink,
Then back to the nest as quick as a wink.
And "Coo," say the little ones, "Coo," says she,
All in their nest on the old pine-tree.

Fast grow the young ones, day and night,
Till their wings are plumed for a longer flight;
Till unto them at last draws nigh
The time when they all must say "Good-by."
Then "Coo," say the little ones, "Coo," says she,
And away they fly from the old pine-tree.

—*Selected.*

CHANGELINGS.

ALONG the orchard's fragrant way
I walked in flower-embroidered May;
The apple-trees were all alight
With opening buds of rose and white.

On the same path I pass again;
The faded grass is wet with rain;
The sweet young year is growing old;
My flowers are changed to globes of gold.

Within the polished spheres there be
Rare honey and rich spicerie;
From sun and wind and blossom bell
The patient days have wrought the spell.
— *M. F. B.* — *Youth's Companion.*

RAGGED ROBIN.

A MAN of taste is Robinet,
   A dandy, spruce and trim!
Whoe'er would dainty fashions set,
   Should go and look at him.

Rob scorns to wear his crimson coat,
   As common people do,
He folds and fits it in and out,
   And does it bravely, too.

Oh! Robin loves to prank him rare,
   With fringe, and flounce, and all;
Till you'd take him for a lady fair
   Just going to a ball.

Robin's a roguish, merry lad,
   He dances in the breeze,
And looks up, with a greeting glad,
   To the rustling hedge-row trees.

How civilly he beckons in
   The busy Mrs. Bee;
And she tells her store of gossiping
   O'er his honey and his glee.

All joy — all mirth — no carking care,
   No worldly woe has he;
Alack! I wish my lot it were
   To live as happily!
                    — *L. A. Twamley.*

THE SONG IN THE STORM.

IT rains, but on a dripping bough
   A little bird sings clear and sweet, —
I think he knows not why nor how,
   Except that with his slender feet
   He feels dear Nature's pulses beat.

The wind, up-rising, stirs the tree,
   And fast with silver tears it weeps;
The little bird more cheerily
   Pipes with his tender throat, and keeps
   His faith in sunshine, tho' it sleeps!

There swings his pretty nest below;
   His mate sits listening to his song;
'Tis love that makes her bosom glow,
   'Tis love that whispers all day long
   "Sleep, sleep, my nestlings, and grow strong!"

Ah, dreary sky, and dripping tree,
   And wind that sobbest in the wood,
Know well, if anywhere love be,

She hath the sunshine in her hood;
For everything to love is good.
   — *James Buckham — Youth's Companion.*

THE GROUND LAUREL.

I LOVE thee, pretty nursling
 Of vernal sun and rain;
For thou art Flora's firstling,
 And leadest in her train.

When far away I found thee,
 It was an April morn;
The chilling blast blew round thee,
 No bud had decked the thorn.

And thou alone wast hiding
 The massy rocks between,
Where, just below them gliding,
 The Merrimac was seen.

And while my hand was brushing
 The seary leaves from thee,
It seemed that thou wast blushing
 To be disclosed to me.

Thou didst reward my ramble
 By shining at my feet,
When, over brake and bramble,
 I sought thy lone retreat.
   — *Miss H. F. Gould.*

A BIRD'S NEST.

OVER my shaded doorway,
  Two little brown-winged birds
Have chosen to fashion their dwelling,
And utter their loving words.
All day they are going and coming
On errands frequent and fleet,
And warbling over and over —
"Sweetest, sweet, sweet, O sweet!"

Their necks are changeful and shining,
Their eyes are like living gems,
And all day long they are busy,
Gathering straws and stems,
Lint and feathers and grasses;
And half forgetting to eat;
Yet never failing to warble,
"Sweetest, sweet, sweet, O sweet!"

I scatter crumbs on the doorsteps,
And fling them some flossy threads;
They fearlessly gather my bounty,
And turn up their graceful heads,
And chatter, and dance, and flutter,
And scrape with their tiny feet,
Telling me, over and over,
"Sweetest, sweet, sweet, O sweet!"

What if the sky is clouded?
What if the rain comes down?
They are all dressed to meet it,
In waterproof suits of brown.

They never mope nor languish
Nor murmur at storm or heat,
But say, — whatever the weather, —
"Sweetest, sweet, sweet, O sweet!" —

Always merry and busy, —
Dear little brown-winged birds,
Teach me the happy magic
Hidden in these soft words,
Which always, in shine or shadow,
So lovingly you repeat
Over, and over, and over,
"Sweetest, sweet, sweet, O sweet!"
— *Florence Percy.*

BROTHER ROBIN.

LISTEN! in the April rain,
    Brother Robin's here again:
Songs like showers come and go;
He is house-building, I know.

Though he finds the old pine-tree
Is not where it used to be,
And the nest he made last year,
Torn and scattered far and near, —

He has neither grief nor care;
Building sites are everywhere:

If one nest is blown away,
Fields are full of sticks and hay.

Though old mousing puss last year,
Ate his little ones, I fear,
And he almost died of fright,
That is all forgotten quite.
—*Mrs. Anderson.*

THE CHIMNEY NEST.

A DAINTY, delicate swallow-feather
   Is all that we now in the chimney trace
Of something that, days and days together,
   With twittering bird-notes filled the place.

Where are you flying now, swallow, swallow?
   Where are you waking the spaces blue?
How many little ones follow, follow,
   Whose wings to strength in the chimney grew?

Deep and narrow, and dark and lonely,
   The sooty place that you nested in;
Over you one blue glimmer only,—
   Say, were there many to make the din?

This is certain, that, somewhere or other,
   Up in the chimney is loosely hung
A queer-shaped nest where a patient mother
   Brooded a brood of tender young.

That here, as in many deserted places,
   Brimming with life for hours and hours,
We miss with the hum a thousand graces,
   Valued the more since no more ours.

Ah! why do we shut our eyes half blindly,
   And close our hearts to some wee things near,
Till He who granted them kindly, kindly
   Gathers them back, that we see and hear,

And know, by the loss of the same grown dearer,
   Naught is so small of his works and ways,
But, holding it tenderly when 'twas nearer,
   Had added a joy to our vanished days?

So, little, delicate swallow-feather,
   Fashioned with care by the Master's hand,
I'll hold you close for your message, whether
   Or not the whole I may understand.
— *Mary Barker Dodge.*

THE ROBIN.

IN the tall elm-tree sat the Robin bright,
   Through the rainy April day,
And he caroled clear with a pure delight,
   In the face of the sky so gray.
And the silver rain through the blossoms dropped,
   And fell on the robin's coat,
And his brave red breast, but he never stopped
   Piping his cheerful note.

For oh, the fields were green and glad,
   And the blissful life that stirred
In the earth's wide breast, was full and warm
   In the heart of the little bird.
The rain-cloud lifted, the sunset light
   Streamed wide over valley and hill;
As the plains of heaven the land grew bright,
   And the warm south wind was still.

Then loud and clear called the happy bird,
   And rapturously he sang,
Till wood and meadow and river side
   With jubilant echoes rang.
But the sun dropped down in the quiet west,
   And he hushed his song at last;
All nature softly sank to rest,
   And the April day had passed.
— *Celia Thaxter.*

DON'T KILL THE BIRDS.

DON'T kill the birds, the pretty birds,
   That sing about your door,
Soon as the joyous spring has come,
   And chilling storms are o'er.
The little birds, how sweet they sing!
   Oh! let them joyous live;
And never seek to take the life
   That you can never give.

Don't kill the birds, the pretty birds,
   That play among the trees;
'Twould make the earth a cheerless place,
   Should we dispense with these.
The little birds, how fond they play!
   Do not disturb their sport;
But let them warble forth their songs,
   Till winter cuts them short.

Don't kill the birds, the happy birds,
   That bless the fields and grove;
So innocent to look upon,
   They claim our warmest love.
The happy birds, the tuneful birds,
   How pleasant 'tis to see!
No spot can be a cheerless place
   Where'er their presence be.
                    — *Colesworthy.*

ANXIETY.

A LITTLE bird sat on the edge of her nest;
   Her yellow-beaks slept as sound as tops;
That day she had done her very best,
   And had filled every one of their little crops;
She had filled her own just over-full,
And hence was feeling a little dull.

"Oh, dear!" she sighed, as she sat with her head
   Sunk in her chest, and no neck at all,

While her crop stuck out like a feather bed
   Turned inside out, and rather small, —
"What shall I do if things don't reform?
I don't know where there's a single worm."

"I've had twenty to-day, and the children five each,
   Besides a few flies, and some very fat spiders,
No one will say I don't do as I preach:
   I'm one of the best of bird providers.
But where's the use? — we want a storm;
I don't know where there's a single worm."

"There's five in my crop," said a wee, wee bird,
   That woke at the sound of his mother's pain,
"I know where there's five." And with that word
   He tucked in his head, and was off again.
"The folly of childhood," sighed his mother,
"Has always been my especial bother."

The yellow-beaks they slept on and on,
   They never had heard of the dread to-morrow;
But the mother sat outside making her moan
   She'll soon have to beg, or steal, or borrow,
For she never can tell the night before
Where she shall find one red worm more.

The fact, as I say, was, she'd had too many;
   She couldn't sleep, and she called it virtue,
Motherly foresight, affection, any
   Name you may call it that will not hurt you;
So it was late when she tucked her head in,
And she slept so late it was almost a sin.

But the little fellow who knew of five,
   Nor troubled his head about any more,

Woke very early, felt quite alive,
  And wanted a sixth to add to his store,
He pushed his mother, the greedy elf,
Then thought he had better try for himself.

When his mother awoke and rubbed her eyes,
  Feeling less like a bird, and more like a mole,
She saw him, — fancy with what a surprise —
  Dragging a huge worm out of a hole!
'Twas of this same hero the proverb took form,
"'Tis the early bird that catches the worm."
— George Macdonald

ROBERT OF LINCOLN.

MERRILY swinging on brier and weed,
  Near to the nest of his little dame,
Over the mountain-side or mead,
  Robert of Lincoln is telling his name;
    " Bob-o'-link, bob-o'-link,
    Spink, spank, spink;
Snug and safe is that nest of ours,
Hidden among the summer flowers.
    Chee, chee, chee."

Robert of Lincoln is gayly drest,
  Wearing a bright black wedding coat;
White are his shoulders, and white his crest;
  Hear him call in his merry note:
    " Bob-o'-link, bob-o'-link,
    Spink, spank, spink;

Look, what a nice new coat is mine,
Sure there was never a bird so fine.
  Chee, chee, chee."

Robert of Lincoln's Quaker wife,
 Pretty and quiet, with plain brown wings,
Passing at home a patient life,
 Broods in the grass, while her husband sings,
  " Bob-o'-link, bob-o'-link,
   Spink, spank, spink;
Brood, kind creature; you need not fear
Thieves and robbers, while I am here.
  Chee, chee, chee."

Modest and shy as a nun is she,
 One weak chirp is her only note,
Braggart and prince of braggarts is he,
 Pouring boasts from his little throat,
  " Bob-o'-link, bob-o'link,
   Spink, spank, spink;
Never was I afraid of man,
Catch me, cowardly knaves, if you can!
  Chee, chee, chee."

Six white eggs on a bed of hay,
 Flecked with purple, a pretty sight!
There as the mother sits all day,
 Robert is singing with all his might:
  " Bob-o'-link, bob-o'link,
   Spink, spank, spink;
Nice good wife, that never goes out,
Keeping house, while I frolic about.
  Chee, chee, chee."

Soon as the little ones chip the shell,
  Six wide mouths are open for food,
Robert of Lincoln bestirs him well,
  Gathering seeds for the hungry brood;
    " Bob-o'-link, bob-o'-link,
      Spink, spank, spink;
This new life is likely to be
Hard for a gay young fellow, like me.
      Chee, chee, chee."

Robert of Lincoln at length is made
  Sober with work and silent with care;
Off is his holiday garment laid,
  Half forgotten that merry air;
    " Bob-o'-link, bob-o'-link,
      Spink, spank, spink;
Nobody knows, but my mate and I,
Where our nest and our nestlings lie.
      Chee, chee, chee."

Summer wanes; the children are grown;
  Fun and frolic no more he knows,
Robert of Lincoln's a humdrum crone;
  Off he flies, and we sing as he goes,
    " Bob-o'-link, bob-o'link,
      Spink, spank, spink;
When you can pipe that merry old strain,
Robert of Lincoln, come back again.
      Chee, chee, chee."
                    — *William Cullen Bryan.*

MARJORIE'S ALMANAC.

ROBINS in the tree-top,
   Blossoms in the grass,
Green things a-growing
   Everywhere you pass;
Sudden little breezes,
   Showers of silver dew,
Black bough and bent twig
   Budding out anew;
Pine-tree and willow-tree,
   Fringéd elm, and larch, —
Don't you think that May-time's
   Pleasanter than March?

Apples in the orchard
   Mellowing one by one;
Strawberries upturning
   Soft cheeks to the sun;
Roses faint with sweetness,
   Lilies fair of face,
Drowsy scents and murmurs
   Haunting every place;
Lengths of golden sunshine,
   Moonlight bright as day, —
Don't you think that summer's
   Pleasanter than May?

Roger in the corn-patch
   Whistling negro songs;
Pussy by the hearth-side
   Romping with the tongs;

Chestnuts in the ashes
  Bursting through the rind;
Red leaf and gold leaf
  Rustling down the wind;
Mother "doin' peaches"
  All the afternoon, —
Don't you think that autumn's
  Pleasanter than June?

Little fairy snow-flakes
  Dancing in the flue;
Old Mr. Santa Claus,
  What is keeping you?
Twilight and firelight
  Shadows come and go;
Merry chime of sleigh-bells
  Tinkling through the snow;
Mother knitting stockings
  (Pussy's got the ball), —
Don't you think that winter's
  Pleasanter than all?
              — *Thomas Bailey Aldrich.*

THE MONKEY.

MONKEY, little merry fellow,
  Thou art Nature's Punchinello!
Full of fun as Puck could be,
Harlequin might learn of thee!

Look now at his odd grimaces!
Saw you ever such queer faces?

Now like learned judge sedate,
Now with nonsense in his pate.

Look now at him! gently peep!
He pretends to be asleep, —
Fast asleep upon his bed,
With his arm beneath his head.

Now that posture is not right,
And he is not settled quite;
There! that's better than before,
And the knave pretends to snore.

Ha! he is not half asleep;
See, he slyly takes a peep!
Monkey, though your eyes were shut,
You could see this little nut.

You shall have it, pigmy brother!
What! another? and another?
Nay, your cheeks are like a sack;
Sit down, and begin to crack.

There! the little ancient man
Cracks as fast as crack he can;
Now good-by, you merry fellow,
Nature's primest Punchinello.

— *Mary Howitt.*

THE PIGEON HOUSE.

LOOK! here's a pretty pigeon house!
   In every narrow cell
A pigeon with his little wife
   And family may dwell.

Their beds are only made of straw,
   The rooms are dark and small;
But many though the pigeons be,
   There's room enough for all.

Because they don't dispute and fret
   For every little thing,
But live in love and gentleness,
   At home and on the wing.

How soft and low their cooing sounds,
   As each one says "Good-night!"
How cheerful when at early morn
   They dress their feathers white.

Then far into the woods and fields,
   To seek their food they fly,
Returning to their house betimes,
   When sunset gilds the sky.

—*Blades and Flowers.*

NOW THE SUN IS SINKING.

NOW the sun is sinking
   In the golden west;
Birds and bees and children
   All have gone to rest;

And the merry streamlet,
  As it runs along,
With a voice of sweetness
  Sings its evening song.

Cowslip, daisy, violet,
  In their little beds,
All among the grasses
  Hide their heavy heads;
Then they'll all, sweet darlings,
  Lie in happy dreams,
Till the rosy morning
  Wakes them with its beams.
                          —*Selected.*

LULLABY.

THROUGH Sleepy-land doth a river flow;
  On its further bank white daisies grow;
And snow-white sheep, in woolly floss,
Must, one by one, be ferried across.
In a little boat they safely ride
To the meadows green, on the other side.
    Lullaby, sing lullaby!

The boatman comes to carry the sheep
In his little boat to the land of sleep;
Upon his head is a poppy wreath;
His eyelids droop, and his eyes beneath
Are drowsy from counting, "One, two, three,"—
How many sheep does the baby see?
    Lullaby, sing lullaby!

One little sheep has gone over the stream,
They press to the bank. How eager they seem!
Two little sheep, alone on the shore, —
Only two sheep, but he's bringing one more;
Three little sheep, in the flowery fields,
Cropping the grass which Sleepy-land yields.
    Lullaby, sing lullaby!

Four little, five little sheep now are over;
Six little, seven little sheep in the clover, —
Deep in the honey-sweet clover they stand.
Eight little, nine little sheep, now they land;
Ten, and eleven, and twelve little sheep! —
And baby, herself, is gone with them to sleep! —
    Lullaby, sing lullaby!
                          — *E. Cavazza — St. Nicholas.*

TWINKLE, TWINKLE, LITTLE STAR.

TWINKLE, twinkle, little star;
   How I wonder what you are!
Up above the world so high,
Like a diamond in the sky.

When the blazing sun is gone,
When he nothing shines upon,
Then you show your little light,
Twinkle, twinkle, all the night.

  In the dark blue sky you keep,
  And often through my curtains peep;
  For you never shut your eye
  Till the sun is in the sky.

And your bright and tiny spark
Lights the traveler in the dark.
Though I know not what you are,
Twinkle, twinkle, little star.
— *Jane Taylor.*

THE STARS ARE COMING.

SEE, the stars are coming
   In the fair blue sky;
Mother, look, they brighten:
   Are they angels' eyes?

No, my child, the lustre
   Of the stars is given,
Like the hues of flowers,
   By the God of heaven.

Mother, if I study,
   Sure he'll make me know
Why the stars he kindled,
   O'er our earth to glow.

Child, what God created
   Has a glorious aim;
Thine it is to worship,
   Thine to love his name.

GOD'S FATHER-CARE.

THERE is no birdling in the nest the breeze rocks in the tree,
All featherless and fluttering, with eyes that cannot see,
But brooding mother-wings are there to keep it snug and warm,
And shelter it most lovingly from sunshine and from storm.

To every flitting butterfly the flower-cups open wide;
Beneath the green leaf's canopy the meanest worm may hide;
Each tiny insect finds or builds some little house or cell,
And in and out goes happily, contented there to dwell.

Now who has thought of all these things? Who planned and made them all?
The One who counts the shining stars, and suffers none to fall;
His tender Father-love is stretched o'er everything we see,
And faileth never, night or day, to care for you and me.
— *After the German of Hey — C. M. Harris.*

SONGS OF SUMMER.

Songs of Summer.

PSALM XXIII.

"The Lord is my shepherd."

THE Lord is my shepherd; I shall not want.
> He maketh me to lie down in green pastures;
> > he leadeth me beside the still waters.
>
> He restoreth my soul; he leadeth me in the
paths of righteousness for his name's sake.

Yea, though I walk through the valley of the shadow of
> death, I will fear no evil; for thou art with me; thy
> rod and thy staff they comfort me.

Thou preparest a table before me in the presence of mine
> enemies; thou anointest my head with oil; my cup
> runneth over.

Surely goodness and mercy shall follow me all the days of
> my life: and I will dwell in the house of the Lord
> for ever.

—Holy Bible.

THE WORKS OF GOD.

GOD made the sky that looks so blue;
> He made the grass so green;

He made the flowers that smell so sweet,
> In pretty color seen.

God made the sun that shines so bright,
    And gladdens all I see;
It comes to give us heat and light;
    How thankful should we be.

God made the pretty bird to fly;
    How sweetly has she sung;
And though she flies so very high,
    She won't forget her young.

God made the cow to give nice milk,
    The horse for me to use;
I'll treat them kindly for His sake,
    Nor dare His gifts abuse.

God made the water for my drink;
    He made the fish to swim;
He made the tree to bear nice fruit;
    Oh, how should I love Him.

—*Taylor.*

THE USE OF FLOWERS.

GOD might have bade the earth bring forth
    Enough for great and small,
The oak tree, and the cedar tree,
    Without a flower at all.

He might have made enough, enough,
    For every want of ours;
For luxury, medicine, and toil,
    And yet have made no flowers.

The ore within the mountain mine
  Requireth none to grow,
Nor doth it need the lotus flower
  To make the river flow.

The clouds might give abundant rain,
  The nightly dews might fall,
And the herb that keepeth life in man
  Might yet have drunk them all.

Then wherefore, wherefore were they made
  All dyed with rainbow light,
All fashion'd with supremest grace,
  Upspringing day and night —

Springing in valleys green and low,
  And on the mountains high,
And in the silent wilderness,
  Where no man passeth by?

Our outward life requires them not,
  Then wherefore had they birth?
To minister delight to man,
  To beautify the earth;

To whisper hope — to comfort man
  Whene'er his faith is dim;
For whoso careth for the flowers
  Will care much more for Him!

— *Mary Howitt.*

WE THANK THEE.

For flowers that bloom about our feet;
  For tender grass, so fresh, so sweet;
For song of bird and hum of bee;
For all things fair we hear or see, —
    Father in heaven, we thank thee!

For blue of stream and blue of sky;
For pleasant shade of branches high;
For fragrant air and cooling breeze;
For beauty of the blooming trees, —
    Father in heaven, we thank thee!

For mother-love and father-care,
For brothers strong and sisters fair;
For love at home and school each day;
For guidance, lest we go astray, —
    Father in heaven, we thank thee!

For thy dear, everlasting arms,
That bear us o'er all ills and harms;
For blessed words of long ago,
That help us now thy will to know, —
    Father in heaven, we thank thee!

—Selected.

A SONG OF SUMMER.

A cuckoo sat on a tree and sang,
  "Summer is coming, coming;"
And a bee crept out of the hive and began
  Lazily humming, humming.

The frogs, from out the rushes and reeds,
   Into the water went splashing;
And the dragon-fly, with his body of green,
   Through the flags went flashing, flashing.

The dormouse put out her head and said,
   "Really the sun shines brighter;"
But the butterfly answered, "Not yet, not yet,"
   And folded his wings up tighter.

But the thrush and the blackbird began to sing
   Ever sweeter and sweeter,
And the grasshopper chirped, and hopped and skipped
   Ever fleeter and fleeter.

The gnats and the chafers began to buzz;
   And the swallows began to chatter;
"We have come from abroad with the summer at last.
   How lazy you are! What's the matter?"

Then the dormouse said, "Summer's really here,
   Since the swallows are homeward coming;"
And the butterfly spread out his wings, and the bee
   Went louder and louder humming.

And suddenly brighter the sun shone out,
   And the clouds away went sailing,
And the sheep nibbled peacefully at the grass,
   And the cow looked over the paling.

Yes, summer had come, and the cuckoo sang
   His song through woodland and hollow;
"The summer is come; if you don't believe me,
   You have only to ask the swallow."

                                      —*Selected.*

MERRY SUNSHINE.

GOOD-MORNING, Merry Sunshine,
   How did you wake so soon?
You've scared the little stars away
   And shined away the moon.
I saw you go to sleep last night
   Before I ceased my playing,
How did you get way over there?
   And where have you been staying?

I never go to sleep, dear child,
   I just go round to see
My little children of the east,
   Who rise and watch for me.
I waken all the birds and bees
   And flowers on my way,
And now come back to see the child
   Who stayed out late at play.
— Selected.

SUMMER TIME.

I LOVE the cheerful summer time,
   With all its birds and flowers,
Its shining garments green and smooth,
   Its cool, refreshing showers.

I love to hear the little birds
   That carol on the trees;
I love the gentle murmuring stream;
   I love the evening breeze.

I love the bright and glorious sun
    That gives us light and heat;
I love the pearly drops of dew
    That sparkle 'neath my feet.

I love to hear the busy hum
    Of honey-making bee,
And learn a lesson, hard to learn,
    Of patient industry.

I love to see the playful lambs,
    So innocent and gay;
I love the faithful, watchful dog
    Who guards them night and day.

I love to think of Him who made
    These pleasant things for me;
Who gave me life and health and strength,
    And eyes that I might see.

I love the holy Sabbath-day,
    So peaceful, calm, and still;
And oh, I love to go to church,
    To learn my Maker's will.

—*Selected.*

THE SUNBEAM.

A LITTLE sunbeam in the sky
    Said to itself one day:
"I'm very small, but why should I
    Do nothing else but play?
I'll go down to the earth and see
If there is any use for me."

The violet beds were wet with dew,
   Which filled each heavy cup;
The little sunbeam darted through,
   And raised their blue heads up;
They smiled to see it, and they lent
The morning's breeze their sweetest scent.

A mother, 'neath a shady tree,
   Had left her babe asleep;
It woke and cried, but when it spied
   The little sunbeam peep
So slyly in, with glance so bright,
It laughed and chuckled with delight.

On, on it went, it might not stay:
   Now through a window small
It poured its glad but tiny ray,
   And danced upon the wall.
A pale young face looked up to meet
The sunbeam she had watched to greet.

And now away beyond the sea
   The merry sunbeam went;
A ship was on the waters free,
   From home and country sent,
But, sparkling in the sunbeam's play,
The blue waves curled around her way.

A voyager stood and watched them there,
   With heart of bitter pain;
She gazed, and half forgot her care,
   And hope came back again.
She said, "The waves are full of glee,
Then yet there may be joy for me!"

And so it traveled to and fro,
  And frisked and danced about;
And not a door was shut, I know,
  To keep the sunbeam out.
But ever, as it touched the earth,
It woke up happiness and mirth.

I may not tell the history
  Of all that it could do,
But I tell you this, that you may try
  To be a sunbeam too;
By little smiles to soothe and cheer,
And make your presence ever dear.

—*Selected.*

LITTLE SUNBEAM.

LITTLE yellow Sunbeam,
  Waking up one day,
Down into the garden
  Took her shining way;
Merrily went dancing
  Down the morning air,
Shaking out the sparkles
  From her golden hair.

Little yellow Sunbeam
  Twinkled all about,
Down among the green leaves
  Flitting in and out.

Waking up the daisies
  From their morning doze,
Ringing up the lily-bells,
  Knocking up the rose.

Little yellow Sunbeam,
  Climbing up the wall,
On the baby's window
  Happened for to fall;
In the little chamber
  As she took a peep,
There she saw the Lovely One
  Lying fast asleep.

Little yellow Sunbeam
  Tripped into the room,
Sweeping out the darkness
  With her golden broom.
All the little shadows,
  Glimmering and gray,
Gathered up their dusky skirts,
  Softly slid away.

Little yellow Sunbeam,
  Flitting to the bed,
Merrily went dancing
  Round the baby's head.
Suddenly there flashed out,
  To her great surprise,
Other little sunbeams
  From the baby's eyes.

Little yellow Sunbeam
  Said, "How can this be?

Whence these little sparklers
  So unlike to me?
Scarce I think they can be
  Sunbeams real and true,
For we all are yellow;
  These are lovely blue."

Little yellow Sunbeam
  Flew back to the sky,
Running to her father,
  She began to cry:
"Father, you must vanish!
  Run and hide your head!
There's a brighter sun than you
  In the baby's bed."
        —*In My Nursery—Laura E. Richards.*

THE FOUR SUNBEAMS.

FOUR little sunbeams came earthward one day,
  Shining and dancing along on their way;
    Resolved that their course should be blest.
"Let us try," they all whispered, "some kindness to do,
Not seek our own pleasuring all the day through,
    Then meet in the eve at the west."

One sunbeam ran in at a low cottage door,
And played "hide-and-seek" with a child on the floor,
    Till baby laughed loud in his glee,
And chased with delight his strange playmate so bright,
The little hands grasping in vain for the light
    That ever before them would flee.

One crept to the couch where an invalid lay,
And brought him a dream of the sweet summer day,
    Its bird-song and beauty and bloom;
Till pain was forgotten and weary unrest,
And in fancy he roamed through the scenes he loved best,
    Far away from the dim, darkened room.

One stole to the heart of a flower that was sad,
And loved and caressed her until she was glad,
    And lifted her white face again;
For love brings content to the lowliest lot,
And finds something sweet in the dreariest spot,
    And lightens all labor and pain.

And one, where a little blind girl sat alone
Not sharing the mirth of her playfellows, shone
    On hands that were folded and pale,
And kissed the poor eyes that had never known sight,
That never would gaze on the beautiful light
    Till angels had lifted the veil.

At last, when the shadows of evening were falling,
And the sun, their great father, his children was calling,
    Four sunbeams sped into the west.
All said, "We have found that in seeking the pleasure
Of others, we fill to the full our own measure,"—
    Then softly they sank to their rest.

— *M. K. B.*

LITTLE NANNIE.

FAWN-FOOTED Nannie,
   Where have you been?
"Chasing the sunbeams
   Into the glen;
Plunging through silver lakes
   After the moon;
Tracking o'er meadows
   The footsteps of June."

Sunny-eyed Nannie,
   What did you see?
"Saw the fays sewing
   Green leaves on a tree;
Saw the waves counting
   The eyes of the stars:
Saw cloud-lambs sleeping
   By sunset's red bars."

Listening Nannie,
   What did you hear?
"Heard the rain asking
   A rose to appear;
Heard the woods tell
   When the wind whistled wrong;
Heard the stream flow
   Where the bird drinks his song."

Nannie, dear Nannie,
   Oh, take me with you,
To run and to listen,
   And see as you do!

"Nay, nay! you must borrow
My ear and my eye,
Or the beauty will vanish,
The music will die."
— *Lucy Larcom.*

A SUMMER DAY.

THIS is the way the morning dawns:
   Rosy tints on flowers and trees,
   Winds that wake the birds and bees,
Dew-drops on the flowers and lawns —
This is the way the morning dawns.

This is the way the sun comes up:
   Gold on brooks and grass and leaves,
   Mist that melts above the sheaves.
Vine and rose and buttercup —
This is the way the sun comes up.

This is the way the rain comes down:
   Tinkle, tinkle, drop by drop,
   Over roof and chimney-top;
Boughs that bend, and clouds that frown —
This is the way the rain comes down.

This is the way the river flows:
   Here a whirl, and there a dance,
   Slowly now, then, like a lance,
Swiftly to the sea it goes —
This is the way the river flows.

This is the way the daylight dies:
　　Cows are lowing in the lane,
　　Fireflies wink o'er hill and plain;
Yellow, red, and purple skies —
This is the way the daylight dies.

　　　　　　　　　　— *Selected.*

MUSIC OF NATURE.

HAVE you heard the waters singing,
　　　　Little May,
Where the willows green are leaning
　　　　O'er their way?
　　Do you know how low and sweet,
　　O'er the pebbles at their feet,
　　Are the words the waves repeat,
　　　　Night and day?

Have you heard the robins singing,
　　　　Little one,
Where the rosy day is breaking —
　　　　When 'tis done?
　　Have you heard the wooing breeze,
　　In the blossomed orchard trees,
　　And the drowsy hum of bees
　　　　In the sun?

All the earth is full of music,
　　　　Little May;
Bird and bee and water singing
　　　　On its way.

Let their silver voices fall
On thy heart with happy call:
"Praise the Lord who loveth all,
Night and day."
— *Selected.*

UNDER THE GREENWOOD TREE.

UNDER the greenwood tree,
Who loves to lie with me,
And tune his merry note
Unto the sweet bird's throat?
Come hither, come hither, come hither;
Here shall we see
No enemy
But winter and rough weather.

Who doth ambition shun,
And loves to live in the sun,
Seeking the food he eats,
And pleased with what he gets?
Come hither, come hither, come hither;
Here shall we see
No enemy
But winter and rough weather.
— *William Shakespeare.*

SUMMER WOODS.

COME ye unto the summer woods
  There entereth no annoy;
All greenly wave the chestnut leaves,
  And the earth is full of joy.

There come the little gentle birds,
  Without a fear of ill,
Down to the murmuring water's edge,
  And freely drink their fill;

And dash about and splash about,
  The merry little things,
And look askance with bright black eyes,
  And flirt their dripping wings.

There's enough for every one,
  And they lovingly agree;
We might learn a lesson all of us,
  Beneath the greenwood tree.
—*Mary Howitt.*

IN THE MEADOW.

THE meadow is a battle-field
  Where summer's army comes;
Each soldier with a clover shield,
  The honey-bees with drums.
Boom, rat-ta! they march, and pass
  The captain tree who stands
Saluting with a sword of grass
  And giving them commands.

'Tis only when the breezes blow
   Across the woody hills,
They shoulder arms, and, to and fro,
   March in their full-dress drills.
Boom, rat-ta! they wheel in line
   And wave their gleaming spears;
"Charge!" cries the captain, giving sign,
   And every soldier cheers.

But when the day is growing dim,
   They gather in their camps
And sing a good thanksgiving hymn
   Around the firefly lamps.
Rat-tat-ta! the bugle-notes
   Call "good-night" to the sky;
I hope they all have overcoats
   To keep them warm and dry.

—Selected.

THE RIVER.

O TELL me, pretty river!
   Whence do thy waters flow?
And whither art thou roaming,
   So pensive and so slow?

"My birthplace was the mountain,
   My nurse, the April showers;
My cradle was a fountain,
   O'ercurtained by wild flowers.

"One morn I ran away,
  A madcap, hoyden rill —
And many a prank that day
  I play'd adown the hill!

"And then, mid meadowy banks,
  I flirted with the flowers
That stoop'd with glowing lips
  To woo me to their bowers.

"But these bright scenes are o'er,
  And darkly flows my wave —
I hear the ocean's roar,
  And there must be my grave!"
  —*Samuel G. Goodrich.*

THE CLOUDS.

HIGH above us, slowly sailing
  Little clouds so soft and white,
You are like the wings of angels,
  Watching o'er us day and night.

When the summer sun is shining
  And the sky is blue above,
Then you look at us and send us
  Radiant smiles of joy and love.

In the morning very early
  From his soft and lowly nest
Soars the lark with joyous carol
  Till he nestles in your breast.

Tender messages he carries
>   From the flowers that watch and sigh
As they gaze upon you sailing,
>   Slowly sailing through the sky.
>   >   —*Selected.*

THE DEW.

"MAMMA," said little Isabel,
>   "While I am fast asleep
The pretty grass and lovely flowers
>   Do nothing else but weep.

"For every morning, when I wake,
>   The glistening tear-drops lie
Upon each tiny blade of grass,
>   And in each flower's eye.

"I wonder why the grass and flowers
>   At night become so sad, —
For early through their tears they smile
>   And seem all day so glad.

"Perhaps 'tis when the sun goes down
>   They fear the gathering shade,
And that is why they cry at night —
>   Because they are afraid.

"Mamma, if I should go and tell
>   The pretty grass and flowers
About God's watchful love and care
>   Through the dark midnight hours, —

"I think they would no longer fear,
 But cease at night to weep;
And then, perhaps they'd bow their heads,
 And gently go to sleep."

"What seemeth tears," the mother said,
 "Is the refreshing dew
Our Heavenly Father sendeth down,
 Each morn and evening new.

"The glittering drops of pearly dew
 Are to the grass and flowers
What slumber through the silent night
 Is to this life of ours.

"Thus God remembers all the works
 That he in love hath made;
O'er all, his watchfulness and care
 Are night and day displayed."
                              — *Selected.*

RAIN IN SUMMER.

O GENTLE, gentle summer rain,
 Let not the silver lily pine,
The drooping lily pine in vain
 To feel that dewy touch of thine,—
To drink thy freshness once again,
O gentle, gentle summer rain!

In heat the landscape quivering lies;
 The cattle pant beneath the tree;

NATURE IN VERSE.

Through parching air and purple skies
   The earth looks up, in vain, for thee;
For thee, — for thee, it looks in vain,
O gentle, gentle summer rain!

Come, then, and brim the meadow streams,
   And soften all the hills with mist,
O falling dew! from burning dreams
   By thee shall herb and flower be kissed,
And Earth shall bless thee yet again,
O gentle, gentle summer rain!
                                 — *W. C. Bennett.*

SUMMER SHOWER.

A DROP fell on the apple-tree,
   Another on the roof;
A half a dozen kissed the eaves,
   And made the gables laugh.

A few went out to help the brook,
   That went to help the sea;
Myself conjectured, were they pearls,
   What necklaces could be!

The dust replaced in hoisted roads,
   The birds jocoser sung;
The sunshine threw his hat away;
   The orchards spangles hung.

The breezes brought dejected lutes,
   And bathed them in the glee;
The East put out a single flag,
   And signed the fête away.
                              — *Emily Dickinson.*

A SONG OF CLOVER.

I WONDER what the Clover thinks —
Intimate friend of Bob-o'-links,
Lover of Daisies slim and white,
Waltzer with Buttercups at night;
Keeper of Inn for traveling Bees,
Serving to them wine dregs and lees,
Left by the Royal Humming Birds,
Who sip and pay with fine-spun words;
Fellow with all the lowliest,
Peer of the gayest and the best;
Comrade of winds, beloved of sun,
Kissed by the Dew-drops, one by one;
Prophet of Good-Luck mystery
By sign of four which few may see;
Symbol of Nature's magic zone,
One out of three, and three in one;
Emblem of comfort in the speech
Which poor men's babies early reach;
Sweet by the roadsides, sweet by rills,
Sweet in the meadows, sweet on hills,
Sweet in its white, sweet in its red, —
Oh, half its sweetness cannot be said; —
Sweet in its every living breath,
Sweetest, perhaps, at last, in death!
Oh! who knows what the Clover thinks?
No one! unless the Bob-o'-links!

—*Saxe Holm.*

PEBBLES.

OUT of a pellucid brook
   Pebbles round and smooth I took;
Like a jewel, every one
Caught a color from the sun, —
Ruby red and sapphire blue,
Emerald and onyx too,
Diamond and amethyst, —
Not a precious stone I missed;
Gems I held from every land
In the hollow of my hand.
Workman Water these had made;
Patiently through sun and shade,
With the ripples of the rill
He had polished them until,
Smooth, symmetrical and bright,
Each one sparkling in the light
Showed within its burning heart
All the lapidary's art;
And the brook seemed thus to sing:
Patience conquers everything!
—Frank Dempster Sherman.

WHAT THE BURDOCK WAS GOOD FOR.

"GOOD for nothing," the farmer said,
   As he made a sweep at the burdock's head;
But then, it was best, no doubt,
To come some day and root her out.

So he lowered his scythe, and went his way,
To see his corn, or gather his hay;
And the weed grew safe and strong and tall,
Close by the side of the garden wall.

"Good for home," cried the little toad,
As he hopped up out of the dusty road.
He had just been having a dreadful fright, —
The boy who gave it was yet in sight.
Here it was cool, and dark, and green,
The safest kind of a leafy screen.
The toad was happy: "For," said he,
"The burdock was plainly meant for me."

"Good for a prop," the spider thought,
And to and fro with care he wrought,
Till he fastened it well to an evergreen
And spun his cables fine between.
'Twas a beautiful bridge, — a triumph of skill,
The flies came 'round as idlers will;
The spider lurked in his corner dim;
The more that came the better for him.

"Good for play," said a child, perplext
To know what frolic was coming next;
So she gathered the burrs that all despised,
And her city playmates were quite surprised
To see what a beautiful basket or chair
Could be made, with a little time and care.
They ranged their treasures about with pride,
And played all day by the burdock's side.

Nothing is lost in this world of ours;
Honey comes from the idle flowers;

The weed which we pass in utter scorn,
May save a life by another morn;
Wonders await us at every turn.
We must be silent and gladly learn,
No room for recklessness or abuse,
Since even a burdock has its use.
—*Selected.*

LILY'S BALL.

LILY gave a party,
   And her little playmates all,
Gayly dressed came in their best,
   To dance at Lily's ball.

Little Quaker Primrose
   Sat and never stirred,
And, except in whispers,
   Never spoke a word.

Snowdrop nearly fainted
   Because the room was hot,
And went away before the rest
   With sweet Forget-me-not.

Pansy danced with Daffodil,
   Rose with Violet;
Silly Daisy fell in love
   With pretty Mignonette.

But, when they danced the country-dance,
   One could scarcely tell
Which of these two danced it best —
   Cowslip or Heatherbell.

Between the dances, when they all
  Were seated in their places,
I thought I'd never seen before
  So many pretty faces.

But, of all the pretty maidens
  I saw at Lily's ball,
Darling Lily was to me
  The sweetest of them all.

And when the dance was over,
  They went downstairs to sup;
Each had a taste of honey-cake,
  With dew in a buttercup.

And all were dressed to go away
  Before the set of sun;
And Lily said "Good-bye," and gave
  A kiss to every one.

Before the moon or a single star
  Was shining overhead,
Lily and all her little friends
  Were fast asleep in bed.
              —*Fun and Earnest.*

PANSY SONG.

OPEN your eyes, my pansies sweet,
  Open your eyes, open to me,
Where did you get your purple hue?
Did a cloud smile as you came through?

Open your eyes, my pansies sweet,
Open your eyes, open to me,
Did a little sunbeam bold
Kiss on your lips that tint of gold?

Open your eyes, my pansies sweet,
Open your eyes, open to me,
Driving away with face so true,
The chilly winds and wintry hue.

Whisper to me, oh pansies sweet,
Tell me, oh, tell me, in rustling low,
Then as I bend with listening ear
Your cheerful voice I plainly hear.
—*Selected.*

THE LILY OF THE VALLEY.

I HAD found out a sweet green spot,
  Where a lily was blooming fair;
The din of the city disturbed it not,
But the spirit that shades the quiet cot
  With its wings of love was there.

I found that lily's bloom,
  When the day was dark and chill;
It smiled like a star in a misty gloom,
And it sent abroad a soft perfume,
  Which is floating around me still.

I sat by the lily's bell,
  And watched it many a day;

The leaves, that rose in a flowing swell,
Grew faint and dim, then drooped and fell,
And the flower had flown away.
— *Percival.*

A CHILD TO A ROSE.

WHITE Rose, talk to me!
   I don't know what to do.
Why do you say no word to me
   Who say so much to you?
I'm bringing you a little rain,
   And I shall feel so proud
If, when you feel it on your face,
   You take me for a cloud.
Here I come so softly
   You cannot hear me walking;
If I take you by surprise
   I may catch you talking.

White Rose, are you tired
   Of staying in one place?
Do you ever wish to see
   The wild flowers, face to face?
Do you know the woodbines,
   And the big brown-crested reeds?
Do you wonder how they live
   So friendly with the weeds?
Have you any work to do
   When you've finished growing?
Shall you teach your little buds
   Pretty ways of blowing?
— *Poems for a Child.*

FORGET-ME-NOT.

WHEN to the flowers — so beautiful —
    The Father gave a name,
Back came a little blue-eyed one
    (All timidly it came)
And standing at its Father's feet,
    And gazing in his face —
It said in low and trembling tones,
    With sweet and gentle grace,
" Dear God, the name thou gavest me
    Alas! I have forgot."
Then kindly looked the Father down,
    And said, " Forget-me-not."

—Selected.

DISCONTENT.

DOWN in a field, one day in June,
    The flowers all bloomed together,
Save one, who tried to hide herself,
    And drooped — that pleasant weather.

A robin, who had flown too high
    And felt a little lazy,
Was resting near the buttercup,
    Who wished she were a daisy.

For daisies grow so trim and tall;
    She always had a passion
For wearing frills around her neck,
    In just the daisies' fashion.

And buttercups must always be
   The same old, tiresome color,
While daisies dress in gold and white,
   Although their gold is duller.

"Dear robin," said this sad young flower,
   "Perhaps you'd not mind trying
To find a nice white frill for me
   Some day, when you are flying."

"You silly thing," the robin said,
   "I think you must be crazy;
I'd rather be my honest self
   Than any made-up daisy.

"You're nicer in your own bright gown;
   The little children love you;
Be the best buttercup you can,
   And think no flower above you.

"Though swallows leave me out of sight,
   We'd better keep our places.
Perhaps the world would all go wrong,
   With one too many daisies.

"Look bravely up into the sky,
   And be content with knowing
That God wished for a buttercup
   Just here, where you are growing."

—*Susan Coolidge.*

GREAT-GRANDMOTHER'S GARDEN.

COME into great-grandmother's garden, my dears,
    The Sunflowers are nodding and beckoning away,
The Balsams are smilingly drying their tears,
    And fair Morning-glories are greeting the day.

How pure is the breath of the old-fashioned Pinks!
    How modest the face of the Lady's Delight!
Sweet William his arm with Miss Lavender's links,
    And whispers, "I dream of you morn, noon, and night."

The Dahlia looks on with a queenly repose,
    Unheeding the Coxcomb's impertinent sighs,
And fierce Tiger-lily an angry look throws
    At Bachelor's Button, who praises her eyes.

The red Prince's Feather waves heavy and slow
    By Marigolds rich as the crown of a king;
The Larkspur the humming-bird sways to and fro;
    Above them the Hollyhocks lazily swing.

Come, Four-o-clocks, wake from your long morning nap!
    The late China Asters will soon be astir;
The Sweet Pea has ordered a simple green cap —
    Which the Poppy considers too common for her.

There's Southernwood, Saffron, and long Stripèd Grass;
    The pale Thimbleberries, the Sweet-brier brush;
An odor of Catnip floats by as we pass —
    Be careful! nor grandmamma's Chamomile crush.

Come into great-grandmother's garden, my dears;
    The Sunflowers are nodding and beckoning away —
The real grandma's garden is gone years and years, —
    We have only a make-believe garden to-day.

                  —*M. J. Jacques—St. Nicholas.*

THE POPPY.

HIGH on a bright and sunny bed
   A scarlet poppy grew;
And up it held its staring head,
   And thrust it full in view.

Yet no attention did it win
   By all these efforts made,
And less unwelcome had it been
   In some retired shade.

For though within its scarlet breast
   No sweet perfume was found,
It seemed to think itself the best
   Of all the flowers around.

From this I may a hint obtain,
   And take great care indeed,
Lest I appear as pert and vain
   As is this gaudy weed.
                      — *Jane Taylor.*

CHORUS OF THE FLOWERS.

I AM the honeysuckle,
   With my drooping head,
And early in the springtime
   I don my dress of red.
I grow in quiet woodlands,
   Beneath some budding tree;
So when you take a ramble
   Just look at me.

I am the dandelion,
  Yellow, as you see,
And when the children see **me**
  They shout for glee.
I grow by every wayside,
  And when I've had my day
I spread my wings so silvery
  And fly away.

When God made all the flowers
  He gave each one a name;
And when the others all had gone
  A little blue one came,
And said, in trembling whisper,
  "My name has been forgot,"
Then the good Father called her
  Forget-me-not.

A fern the people call me,
  I'm always clothed in green;
I live in every forest—
  You've seen me oft, I ween.
Sometimes I leave the shadow
  To grow beside the way;
You'll see me as you pass
  Some nice fine day.

I am the gay nasturtium,
  I bloom in gardens fine;
Among the grander flowers
  My slender stalk I twine.
Bright orange is my color
  The eyes of all to please.
I have a tube of honey
  For all the bees.

I am the little violet
　　In my purple dress;
I hide myself so safely
　　That you'd never guess
There was a flower so near you,
　　Nestling at your feet;
And that is why I send you
　　My fragrance sweet.
　　　　　　　—*Lucy Wheelock.*

FASHIONS AT THE COURT OF QUEEN FLORA.

"OH, pray, do you know of those wonderful styles
　　To be worn with the sweetest and rarest of smiles,
At Queen Flora's court, at receptions in spring,
When each one comes out in the latest new thing?
The modiste who designs all these beautiful things
Is called Fairy Nature, and her artists she brings
From the north and the south, and the east and the west,
And selects from all of their works what is best.

"Of her artists the greatest is named Mr. Sun,
His lights and his shadows can be equaled by none;
And his palette of colors, in rainbows and flowers,
And bright sunset clouds and the fragrant rose-bowers,
Have bewildered and baffled all mortals who tried
To copy his work, but at failure have sighed.
This artist provides cloth-of-gold for the queen;
And from dewdrops, makes diamonds, or emeralds green.

"In green satin tunics the Grasses appear,
While the Leaves change their robes several times in the year;
In the spring they wear shades of most delicate green,
But in autumn in crimson and yellows are seen.
The first little Snowdrops are wrapped in white down,
While the Crocus sprite ventures forth in a silk gown.
But the Tulips wear mantles of purple and gold,
Over robes of rich crimson, as the air is still cold.

"Pale mauve, or soft pink, is the Hyacinth's shade,
In the shape of a bell is her graceful skirt made,
With a girdle of green, and a hat of pale rose,
She's in truth quite a belle at the court, I suppose.
Rich, purple-hued velvets the Pansy maids wear
While cunning caps rest on their long yellow hair.
The tall graceful Lilies are dressed all in white,
With crowns of pure gold, most dazzlingly bright.

"Miss Daisy wears bodice of gold-colored silk,
And skirts slashed in points of gauze white as milk,
And sash of brown velvet with cap of the same,
In truth — a dear daisy — in looks as in name.
In bright scarlet gowns all the Poppies appear,
With pale green-colored hose, and bonnets so queer!
They nod their small heads with expression so wise —
It would seem to be thought — but for sleep in their eyes.

"At summer receptions the Rose sprites appear,
Soft satins, pink, white, or gold-colored they wear,
With bodices trimmed with pink moss buds and leaves,
And mantles of bright light that Mr. Sun weaves.

The Forget-me-nots dance in robes of pale blue,
And the Violets and Blue-bells wear this color too,
While the dear little Clover sprites in pink or white,
Play hide-and-seek with each other in shadow or light.

" When dust soils these toilets, lest their beauty should wane,
They are freshened and cleaned by one Mr. Rain;
And at evening receptions an artist most rare,
By name, a Miss Moonlight, arranges with care
And with marvelous skill all the costumes so bright;
And in her work both mortals and fairies delight;
For she softens gay colors and fair faces too,
And can sometimes make old things appear almost new.

" There are rich gallant lords, and fair ladies, of course,
At Queen Flora's court; and a well-ordered force
Of uniformed troops — the Oaks and the Pines —
Who guard her dominions so rich in rare mines.
The Pines wear green uniforms all days in the year,
But the Oaks and the Maples in gay colors appear
At the autumn receptions, so brilliant and grand,
Ere King Winter has driven them out of the land."
— *Lydia Hoyt Farmer.*

WHO WAS SHE?

I WAS going down the walk,
   So pleasant, cool, and shady;
Right in the middle of the path
   I met a little lady.

I made to her my sweetest bow;
   She only walked on faster.
I smiled, and said "Good-morning, ma'am!"
   The moment that I passed her.

She never noticed me at all;
   I really felt quite slighted.
I thought, "I'll follow you, I will,
   Altho' I'm not invited."

Perhaps you think me very rude;
   But then, she looked so funny —
From head to foot all dressed in fur,
   This summer day so sunny.

She didn't mind the heat at all,
   But wrapped the fur around her,
And hurried on, as if to say,
   "I'll 'tend to my own gown, sir!"

I followed her the whole way home;
   Her home was in my garden,
Beneath my choicest vines — and yet,
   She never asked my pardon.

I never heard her speak a word;
   But once I heard the miller,
Coming down the sidewalk, say,
   "There goes Miss Caterpillar!"

—*Selected.*

THE BUTTERFLY.

OUT in the garden wee Elsie
   Was gathering flowers for me;
"O mamma!" she cried, "hurry, hurry!
   Here's something I want you to see."
I went to the window; before her
   A velvet-winged butterfly flew,
And the pansies themselves were not brighter
   Than the beautiful creature in hue.

"Oh! isn't it pretty!" cried Elsie,
   With eager and wondering eyes,
As she watched it soar lazily upward
   Against the soft blue of the skies.
"I know what it is, don't you, mamma?"—
   Oh! the burden of these little things
When the soul of a poet is in them—
   "It's a pansy—a pansy with wings."

—*Selected.*

THE BUTTERFLY'S LESSON.

THE lilies were swinging their fair, white bells,
   In the languid heat of the noon,
When Golden-wing stopped for a sip of dew,
   One beautiful day in June.

Around lay the gardens, as fair as a rose,
   With blossoms of brightest dyes;
Above in the tree-tops so tall and green,
   Was the home of the birds near the skies.

And Golden-wing thought if he only might live
   On that wind-blown, swaying bough,
He would give up his lilies and honey and dew,
   And be happier, far, than now.

So he fluttered his dainty, golden wings
   And sprang on a passing breeze,
And floated up with a swelling heart,
   To the home of the birds in the trees.

The journey was long, he grew weary and faint,
   The most of his strength was spent;
But still he pressed up to the nest in the trees,
   Urged on by his discontent.

He reached it at last, the pretty, cool nest,
   Where the young birds were learning to sing;
But he was not there long, for a greedy young bird
   Caught sight of poor Golden-wing.

The birds all came rushing in hot pursuit,
   And Golden-wing, faint with fear,
Wished in his trembling, foolish heart,
   That the garden were only near.

And at length, when he reached it, the garden fair,
   And hid in his lily home,
He vowed to be more contented henceforth,
   And never again to roam.

And he learned the lesson we all must heed,
   Whether or not we please,
That those who are made for the lily bells,
   Can never find homes in the trees.

—Selected.

THE GRASSHOPPER.

A GRASSHOPPER sat in an oak tree green,
  Mending the shoes of the fairy queen,
For he was a cobbler of all the fays,
Yellows and purples and greens and grays;
A happy old fellow and merry was he
As he sat on the limb of the old oak tree;
Oh, merry and bold and ever so old,
As I heard one day when this story was told!

A bobolink skirmishing over the way,
Called to the grasshopper, "Sir, good-day!"
And the grasshopper cobbling still at his shoe,
Answered politely, "The same to you!"
And nodded his head with a little bow,
Though I couldn't exactly tell you how;
For the prince of good manners — the grasshopper — he,
As he cobbled away in his old oak tree!

"How much do you make by the day and the week?"
The bobolink asked with a flirt and a shriek;
"Three golden leaves of the buttercup's flower —
Three crystal drops from the latest shower;
Three sacks of meal from the pollen's best
That the elves shake off from the cowslip's breast;
And that doth keep me both well and good —
For I'm the boss cobbler of all the wood!"

A barefoot boy, as he came along,
Had loitered to list to the bobolink's song,
And shy a stone, as well as he could,
At the little boss cobbler of all the wood;

"You cobble a shoe!" he cried as he laughed,
"You're the funniest cobbler of all your craft;
Why, your leather's a leaf, and your paste — it is dew!
Oh, what a cobbler to cobble a shoe!"

But the bobolink answered with honest wrath,
As he peered at the boy in the woodland path,
"Each one is wisest and skillfulest, too,
That knows just the work that he has to do;
For elfin feet those slippers are best,
That are made from the tiniest leaflet's vest;
While Nature's leather seems fitted for you,
As you wear it still!" And away he flew.
— *Independent.*

THE SONG OF THE BEE.

BUZZ! buzz! buzz!
    This is the song of the bee.
His legs are of yellow;
A jolly, good fellow,
    And yet a great worker is he.

In days that are sunny
He's getting his honey;
In days that are cloudy
    He's making his wax:
On pinks and on lilies,
And gay daffodillies,
And columbine blossoms,
    He levies a tax!

Buzz! buzz! buzz!
The sweet-smelling clover,
He, humming, hangs over;
The scent of the roses
   Makes fragrant his wings:
He never gets lazy;
From thistle and daisy,
And weeds of the meadow,
   Some treasure he brings.

Buzz! buzz! buzz!
From morning's first light
Till the coming of night,
He's singing and toiling
   The summer day through.
Oh! we may get weary,
And think work is dreary;
'Tis harder by far
   To have nothing to do.
—*Marian Douglass.*

THE BUSY BEE.

HOW doth the little busy bee
   Improve each shining hour,
And gather honey all the day
   From every opening flower!

How skillfully she builds her cell,
   How neat she spreads the wax!
And labors hard to store it well
   With the sweet food she makes.

In works of labor or of skill,
  I would be busy, too;
For Satan finds some mischief still
  For idle hands to do.

In books, or work, or healthful play,
  Let my first years be past,
That I may give for every day
  Some good account at last.
— Isaac Watts

THE MOCKING-BIRD'S SONG.

EARLY on a pleasant day,
  In the poet's month of May
Field and forest looked so fair,
So refreshing was the air,
That in spite of morning dew,
Forth I walked where tangling grew
Many a thorn and breezy bush;
When the redbreast and the thrush
Gayly raised their early lay,
Thankful for returning day.

Every thicket, bush, and tree
Swelled with grateful harmony;
As it mildly swept along,
Echo seemed to catch the song;
But the plain was wide and clear —
Echo never whispered near;
From a neighboring mocking-bird
Came the answering notes I heard.

Soft and low the song began —
I scarcely caught it as it ran
Through the melancholy trill
Of the plaintive whip-poor-will;
Through the ring-dove's gentle wail,
Chattering jay and whistling quail,
Sparrow's twitter, catbird's cry,
Redbreast's whistle, robin's sigh;
Blackbird, bluebird, swallow, lark,
Each his native note might mark.

Oft he tried the lesson o'er,
Each time louder than before;
Burst at length the finished song,
Loud and clear it poured along;
All the choir in silence heard,
Hushed before this wondrous bird.
All transported and amazed,
Scarcely breathing, long I gazed.

Now it reached the loudest swell;
Lower, lower, now it fell,
Lower, lower, lower still,
Scarce it sounded o'er the rill,
Now the warbler ceased to sing;
Then he spread his russet wing,
And I saw him take his flight,
Other regions to delight.

—*J. R. Drake.*

SUPPOSE.

How dreary would the meadows be
   In the pleasant summer light,
Suppose there wasn't a bird to sing,
   And suppose the grass was white!

And dreary would the garden be
   With all its flowery trees,
Suppose there were no butterflies,
   And suppose there were no bees.

And what would all the beauty be,
   And what the song that cheers,
Suppose we hadn't any eyes,
   And suppose we hadn't ears?

For though the grass were gay and green,
   And song-birds filled the glen,
And the air were purple with butterflies,
   What good would they do, then?

Ah, think of it, my little friends,
   And when some pleasure flies,
Why, let it go, and still be glad
   That you have your ears and eyes.
                  — *Alice Cary.*

OUT-OF-DOOR ARITHMETIC.

Add bright buds, and sun and flowers,
   New green leaves, and fitful showers
To a bare world, and the sum
Of the whole, to spring will come.

Multiply these leaves by more,
And the flowers by a score,
The result, if found aright,
Will be summer, long and bright.

Then divide the flowers, and soon
By gray clouds and storms begun,
And the quotient sure will be
Autumn over land and sea.

From this, then, subtract the red
Of the leaves up overhead.
Also every flower in sight,
And you've winter, cold and bright.
—*Selected.*

LETTING THE OLD CAT DIE.

NOT long ago I wandered near
   A playground in the wood;
And there heard words from a youngster's lips
   That I never quite understood.

"Now let the old cat die!" he laughed.
   I saw him give a push,
Then gayly scamper away as he spied
   A face peep over the bush.

But what he pushed, or where he went,
   I could not well make out,
On account of the thicket of bending boughs
   That bordered the place about.

"The little villain has stoned a cat,
  Or hung it upon a limb,
And left it to die all alone," I said;
  "But I'll play the mischief with him."

I forced my way through the bending boughs
  The poor old cat to seek;
But what did I find but a swinging child,
  With her bright hair brushing her cheek!

Her bright hair floated to and fro,
  Her little red dress flashed by;
But the loveliest thing of all, I thought,
  Was the gleam of her laughing eye.

Swinging and swinging, back and forth,
  With the rose-light in her face,
She seemed like a bird and flower in one,
  And the forest her native place.

"Steady! I'll send you up, my child;"
  But she stopped me with a cry, —
"Go 'way, go 'way! don't touch me, please;
  I'm letting the old cat die."

"You're letting him die!" I cried aghast;
  "Why, where's the cat, my dear?"
And, lo! the laugh that filled the wood
  Was a thing for the birds to hear.

"Why, don't you know," said the little maid,
  The sparkling, beautiful elf, —
"That we call it letting the old cat die
  When the swing stops all itself?"

Then, swinging and swinging and looking back
  With the merriest look in her eye,
She bade me good-bye, and I left her alone,
  Letting the old cat die.
                              — *Selected.*

THE SPIDER AND THE FLY.

"Will you walk into my parlor?"
  Said a spider to a fly;
"'Tis the prettiest little parlor
  That ever you did spy.
The way into my parlor
  Is up a winding stair,
And I have many pretty things
  To show you when you're there."
"O no, no," said the little fly,
  "To ask me is in vain;
For who goes up your winding stair
  Can ne'er come down again."

"I'm sure you must be weary
  With soaring up so high;
Will you rest upon my little bed?"
  Said the spider to the fly.
"There are pretty curtains drawn around;
  The sheets are fine and thin;
And if you like to rest awhile,
  I'll snugly tuck you in."
"O no, no," said the little fly,
  "For I've often heard it said
They never, never wake again,
  Who sleep upon your bed."

NATURE IN VERSE.

Said the cunning spider to the fly,
  "Dear friend, what shall I do
To prove the warm affection
  I've always felt for you?
I have, within my pantry,
  Good store of all that's nice;
I'm sure you're very welcome —
  Will you please to take a slice?"
"O no, no," said the little fly,
  "Kind sir, that cannot be;
I've heard what's in your pantry,
  And I do not wish to see."

"Sweet creature," said the spider,
  "You're witty and you're wise;
How handsome are your gauzy wings,
  How brilliant are your eyes.
I have a little looking-glass
  Upon my parlor shelf;
If you'll step in one moment, dear,
  You shall behold yourself."
"I thank you, gentle sir," she said,
  "For what you're pleased to say,
And bidding you good-morning now,
  I'll call another day."

The spider turned him round about,
  And went into his den,
For well he knew the silly fly
  Would soon be back again;
So he wove a subtle web
  In a little corner sly,
And set his table ready
  To dine upon the fly.

He went out to his door again,
   And merrily did sing,
"Come hither, hither, pretty fly,
   With pearl and silver wing;
Your robes are green and purple,
   There's a crest upon your head;
Your eyes are like the diamond bright,
   But mine are dull as lead."

Alas, alas! how very soon
   This silly little fly,
Hearing his wily, flattering words,
   Came slowly flitting by;
With buzzing wings she hung aloft,
   Then near and nearer drew —
Thought only of her brilliant eyes,
   And green and purple hue;
Thought only of her crested head —
   Poor foolish thing! At last
Up jumped the cunning spider,
   And fiercely held her fast.

He dragged her up his winding stair,
   Into his dismal den
Within his little parlor — but
   She ne'er came out again!
And now, dear little children
   Who may this story read,
To idle, silly, flattering words,
   I pray you, ne'er give heed.
Unto an evil counselor
   Close heart and ear and eye;
And take a lesson from this tale
   Of the spider and the fly.

— Mary Howitt.

O LARK OF THE SUMMER MORNING.

I LOVE to lie in the clover,
   With the lark like a speck in the sky,
While its small, sweet throat runneth over
   With praise it sendeth on high.

O lark of the summer morning,
   Teach, teach me the song that you sing,
I would learn without lightness or scorning,
   To give praise for every good thing.

O lark of the summer morning!
   Give, give me of praying the key,
And I'll learn without lightness or scorning
   As I did at my own mother's knee.
                        —*From the Japanese.*

THE PEACOCK.

COME, come, Mister Peacock, you must not be proud,
   Although you can boast such a train;
For many a bird far more highly endowed
   Is not half so conceited and vain.

Let me tell you, gay bird, that a suit of fine clothes
   Is a sorry distinction at most,
And seldom much valued, excepting by those
   Who such graces only can boast.

The nightingale certainly wears a plain coat,
  But she cheers and delights with her song;
While you, though so vain, cannot utter a note
  To please by the use of your tongue.

The hawk cannot boast of a plumage so gay,
  But piercing and clear is her eye;
And while you are strutting about all the day,
  She gallantly soars in the sky.

The dove may be clad in a plainer attire,
  But she is not so selfish and cold;
And her love and affection more pleasure inspire,
  Than all your fine purple and gold.

So you see, Mister Peacock, you must not be proud,
  Although you can boast such a train;
For many a bird is more highly endowed,
  And not half so conceited and vain.
              —*Songs for the Little Ones at Home.*

NURSERY SONG.

As I walked over the hill one day,
  I listened, and heard a mother-sheep say,
"In all the green world there is nothing so sweet
As my little lammie, with his nimble feet;
      With his eyes so bright,
      And his wool so white,
Oh! he is my darling, my heart's delight,"

And the mother-sheep and her little one
Side by side lay down in the sun;
And they went to sleep on the hillside warm,
While my little lammie lies here on my arm.

I went to the kitchen, and what did I see
But the old gray cat with her kittens three!
I heard her whispering soft; said she,
"My kittens, with tails so cunningly curled,
Are the prettiest things that can be in the world.
   The bird on the tree,
   And the old ewe — she,
   May love their babies exceedingly,
   But I love my kittens there,
   Under the rocking chair.
I love my kittens with all my might,
I love them at morning, noon, and night,
Now I'll take up my kitties, the kitties I love,
And we'll lie down together beneath the warm stove."
Let the kittens sleep under the stove so warm,
While my little darling lies here on my arm.

I went to the yard, and I saw the old hen
Go clucking about with her chickens ten;
She clucked and she scratched and she bustled away,
And what do you think I heard the hen say?
I heard her say, "The sun never did shine
On anything like to these chickens of mine!
You may hunt the full moon and the stars if you please,
But you never will find ten such chickens as these;
My dear downy darlings, my sweet little things,
Come, nestle now cosily under my wings."

So the hen said,
And the chickens all sped,
As fast as they could, to their nice feather bed,
And there let them sleep in their feathers so warm,
While my little chick lies here on my arm.
— *Mrs. Carter.*

IN THE SWING.

HERE we go to the branches high!
   Here we come to the grasses low!
For the spiders and flowers and birds and I
   Love to swing when the breezes blow.
Swing, little bird, on the topmost bough;
   Swing, little spider, with rope so fine;
Swing, little flower, for the wind blows now,
   But none of you have such a swing as mine.

Dear little bird, come sit on my toes;
   I'm just as careful as I can be;
And oh, I tell you, nobody knows
   What fun we'd have if you'd play with me!
Come and swing with me, birdie dear,
   Bright little flower, come swing in my hair;
But you, little spider, creepy and queer, —
   You'd better stay and swing over there!

The sweet little bird, he sings and sings,
   But he doesn't even look in my face;
The bright little blossom swings and swings,
   But still it swings in the self-same place.

Let them stay where they like it best;
   Let them do what they'd rather do;
My swing is nicer than all the rest,
   But maybe it's rather small for two.

Here we go to the branches high!
   Here we come to the grasses low!
For the spiders and flowers and birds and I
   Love to swing when the breezes blow.
Swing, little bird, on the topmost bough;
   Swing, little spider, with rope so fine;
Swing little flower, for the wind blows now;
   But none of you have such a swing as mine.
               — *Eudora S. Bumstead — St. Nicholas.*

GOOD-NIGHT AND GOOD-MORNING.

A FAIR little girl sat under a tree,
   Sewing as long as her eyes could see;
Then smoothed her work and folded it right,
And said, — "Dear work, good-night, good-night!"

Such a number of crows came over her head,
Crying "Caw, caw!" on their way to bed,
She said, as she watched their curious flight,
"Little black things, good-night, good-night!"

The horses neighed, and the oxen lowed,
The sheep's "Bleat, bleat!" came over the road;
All seeming to say, with a quiet delight,
"Good little girl, good-night, good-night!"

She did not say to the sun, " Good-night ! "
Though she saw him there like a ball of light;
For she knew he had God's time to keep
All over the world, and never could sleep.

The tall, pink fox-glove bowed his head;
The violets curtsied, and went to bed;
And good little Lucy tied up her hair,
And said, on her knees, her favorite prayer.

And, while on her pillow she softly lay,
She knew nothing more till again it was day;
And all things said to the beautiful sun,
"Good-morning, good-morning; our work is begun!"
— *Lord Houghton.*

THE BANK-SWALLOWS.

IN a village of Bank-Swallows
   You will find so many a nest,
"That you scarce can tell their number
   Nor which one of them is best."

In the sand-hill, see the openings,
   Round or oval, odd-shaped, some,
Size and form depending, often,
   On how loose the sands become.

When with their short bills they pecked it,
   Clinging fast with claws the while,
Till they made an open doorway
   Suiting them in size and style.

Once within, they peck and peck it, —
   Sometimes quite a yard or more,
While the nest is snugly builded,
   Farthest from the outer door.

But, so wise are they, this archway,
   From the entrance to the nest,
Is inclining ever upward,
   That no rain within may rest.

So the pink-white eggs are laid there,
   Safe from harm, till baby-birds
Chirrup forth to take their places,
   'Mongst the self-sustaining herds.

Parent-birds care less for young ones,
   Than do other swallow-kind ; —
Push them off half-fledged and timid,
   Each his food and home to find.

Thus they, many a time, fall prey to
   Hawks and crows, — their enemies ; —
Even the nest sometimes is entered
   By the snakes and fleas and flies.

Swallows migrate in the winter,
   From the cold to warmer climes, —
Flying back as spring approaches,
   To the haunts of former times.

"Ne'er one swallow makes a summer,"
   Is a saying everywhere ;
But when swallows come in myriads,
   Blessed summer-time is here.

—Selected.

THREE O'CLOCK IN THE MORNING.

WHAT do the robins whisper about
    From their homes in the elms and birches?
I've tried to study the riddle out,
But still in my mind is many a doubt,
  In spite of deep researches.

While over the world is silence deep,
   In the twilight of early dawning,
They begin to chirp and twitter and peep,
As if they were talking in their sleep,
  At three o'clock in the morning.

Perhaps the little ones stir and complain
   That it's time to be up and doing;
And the mother-bird sings a drowsy strain
To coax them back to their dreams again,
  Though distant cocks are crowing.

Or do they tell secrets that should not be heard
   By mortals listening and prying?
Perhaps we might learn from some whispering word
The best way to bring up a little bird —
  Or the wonderful art of flying.

It may be they speak of an autumn day,
   When, with many a feathered roamer,
Under the clouds so cold and gray,
Over the hill they take their way,
  In search of the vanished summer.

It may be they gossip from nest to nest,
   Hidden and leaf-enfolded;

For do we not often hear it confessed,
When a long-kept secret at last is guessed,
   That "a little bird has told it"?

Perhaps — but the question is wrapped in doubt,
   They give me no hint or warning.
Listen, and tell me if you find out
What do the robins talk about
   At three o'clock in the morning.
                  — *R. S. Palfrey.*

WHO STOLE THE BIRD'S NEST?

"TO-WHIT, to-whit, to-whee!
   Will you listen to me?
Who stole four eggs I laid,
And the nice nest I made?"

"Not I," said the cow; "moo-oo!
Such a thing I'd never do.
I gave you a wisp of hay,
But didn't take your nest away.
Not I," said the cow; "moo-oo!
Such a thing I'd never do!"

"Bob-o'-link! bob-o'-link!
Now, what do you think?
Who stole a nest away
From the plum-tree to-day?"

"Not I," said the dog; "bow-wow!
I wouldn't be so mean anyhow.
I gave hairs the nest to make,
But the nest I did not take.
Not I," said the dog; "bow-wow!
I wouldn't be so mean anyhow!"

"Coo-coo, coo-coo, coo-coo!
Let me speak a word or two:
Who stole that pretty nest
From little yellow breast?"

"Not I," said the sheep; "oh, no!
I wouldn't treat a poor bird so.
I gave wool the nest to line,
But the nest was none of mine.
Baa, baa!" said the sheep; "oh, no!
I wouldn't treat a poor bird so!"

"Caw, caw!" cried the crow;
"I should like to know
What thief took away
A bird's nest to-day?"

"Chick, chick!" said the hen;
"Don't ask me again;
Why, I haven't a chick
Would do such a trick!
We each gave her a feather
And she wove them together.
I'd scorn to intrude
On her and her brood.
Cluck, cluck!" said the hen;
"Don't ask me again."

"Chir-a-whir! chir-a-whir!
We'll make a great stir,
And find out his name,
And all cry, 'For shame!'"

"I would not rob a bird,"
  Said little Mary Green;
"I think I never heard
  Of anything so mean."

"It is very cruel too,"
  Said little Alice Neal;
"I wonder if he knew
  How sad the bird would feel!"

A little boy hung down his head,
And went and hid behind the bed;
For he stole that pretty nest,
From poor little yellow breast;
And he felt so full of shame,
He didn't like to tell his name.
  —*L. Maria Child.*

THE PETER-BIRD.

WHEN summer's birds are bringing
    Their clear, concerted singing,
Singing gladder, gladder, gladder in their glees;
    When finches and the thrushes
    Make vocal all the bushes,
And the lark his note of morning welcome frees —
    I hear no meter sweeter
    Than "Peter — Peter — Peter,"
That the Peter-bird is singing in my trees.

How good to lie and listen,
Where brooks in summer glisten,
As they ripple, ripple, ripple to the seas;
Where faintly in the pebbles
They play their pretty trebles
In the plaintive, sad, and tender minor keys;
But they can play no meter
Like " Peter — Peter — Peter,"
That the Peter-bird is singing in my trees.

When softly at the nooning
I hear the clover crooning
Of its nectar, nectar, nectar, and the bees;
When corn a-field is drying,
And fading blades are flying
With a floating pennon-rustle in the breeze,
Oh, sweet it is, but sweeter
Is " Peter — Peter — Peter,"
That the Peter-bird is singing in my trees.

When summer's joy is over
And bees have robbed the clover,
Leaving odor, only odor, to appease;
When red autumnal juices
Make music in their sluices
As the fruity currents gurgle from their lees;
The wine-tide sings not sweeter
Than " Peter — Peter — Peter,"
That the Peter-bird is singing in my trees.

—*Henry Thompson Stanton*—*Century, Aug.* 1889.

A FABLE.

I KNOW not what sly little fairy
    Crept into the woods that day,
But every birdie tried singing,
    Each in his neighbor's way.

Said Robin, "I'm tired of shouting
    My loud notes the whole day through,
I'll warble softly and sweetly,
    Like my neighbor dressed in blue."

Said Bluebird, "I'm tired of singing
    My poor little piping song;
I'll make my notes like the robin's,
    Saucy, and bold and strong."

Said Bobolink, ceasing his singing
    Atop of a blossoming spray,
"I'm sick of my tinkling nonsense,
    I'll sing like the thrush to-day."

Said the Thrush, "I'm tired of lisping
    Sad notes to these shadows dark,
I'll hie me away to the meadows
    And merrily sing like the lark."

Bobolink began; — such an odd little noise;
    Said the solemn pine-trees, "Hush!
You're just a saucy meadow bird,
    You never will be a thrush."

The thrush and robin and bluebird!
    You ought to have heard the brook
Laugh at their queer performances;
    The grasses bent double and shook.

Their airy heads with laughter,
  The daisies stared and blushed
For their friends, the little musicians.
  Just then the gray sky flushed,

And the sun came up to the rescue,
  Wearing his comforting smile,
" My dears," he said, " this nonsense
  Is never worth your while.

" Go each and attend to singing
  Your own sweet song of praise,
There's naught in the world so foolish
  As aping your neighbor's ways."
        — *Popular Educator.*

THE BIRDS' LAWN PARTY.

THE birds of the woodland, in soft summer weather,
  Once gave a lawn party, way down in the heather.

Their neat invitations were written, you see,
On the prettiest leaves from the prettiest tree.

Then daintily tied with a fine silver thread,
And gracefully hung round a carrier-dove's head,

Who sped on her mission with a joyful glee,
And delivered each note with an " R. S. V. P."

To flowers and insects and plants, one and all,
Were sent invitations to attend the grand ball.

The night soon arrived, and the moon shone so bright,
That the birds sang together in happy delight.

The Bullfrogs and Tree-toads, who lived very near,
In new coats of green satin were first to appear.

Then followed musicians, a numerous band
Who were led by Mosquitoes from Cedar Swamp Land.

The Beetle came in with Miss Grasshopper Green;
Then Crickets and Flies were the next to be seen.

That the Wasp and the Spider, both stylishly dressed,
Were the most graceful dancers, by all was confessed.

There were Robin Redbreast and dear Jennie Wren;
Causing all the Magpies to chatter again.

And the Nightingale, too, in a loving refrain,
Was wooing the Dove, his old sweetheart, again;

While lingering near, in a blackberry bush,
Was the silver-tongued Linnet, and fair bride, the Thrush

Now who do you think the chaperons there!
Why, the three Mrs. Owls, from Dismal Swamp Square.

The flowers and plants, though the last to appear,
Wore the loveliest costumes of any one there.

With just one exception — the Butterflies gay,
Whose costumes are made by the fairies, they say.

The Daisies were peerless in robes of pure white,
And their proud, happy mothers looked on in delight.

The Buttercups followed, of riches untold,
For each was arrayed in a gown of pure gold;

And the Clovers looked sweet in pale pink and white,
As they merrily danced in the moon's silver light.

The Rosebud, the fairest, and queen of them all,
Was acknowledged the belle of this beautiful ball.

The music was charming, the feast was quite grand;
There were sweetmeats enough for all guests in the land.

For each little flower who daintily sups,
The Fairies served dewdrops in lily-bell cups.

The dancing continued, the merriment, too,
Till the Moon became weary, and softly withdrew.

The Fireflies said they would serve in her place,
Since the Moon had so selfishly hidden her face.

Then the three Mrs. Owls from guest to guest flew,
Said, " The Moon has retired; I think we must, too."

The Fireflies came with their swift-flashing light,
And escorted the flowers and plants home that night.

All the guests bade adieu, and their homeward way wended,
From the nicest affair they had ever attended.
— *Child Garden.*

THE HAPPY BIRD.

OH, if I were a little bird
    Happy would I be,
Perched all day on a leafy tree;
Oh, down in the meadow
Drinking in the dew,
I'd be a merry bird, say, wouldn't you?

Not a single grammar lesson,
Not a word to spell,
Funny old schoolhouse
Without any bell!
Oh, a cherry for a lunch
And a blossom for a book
And a dinner with the honey bee,
Down by the brook.
— Selected.

THE HIDDEN SONGSTER.

HARK! Hear you not that long, shrill strain?
    Where is the singer hid?
I've looked, and looked, but all in vain.
    Where are you? "Katy-did,"

Comes back in answer to my call.
    "Did what? Did what?" I cry.
But "Katy-did," and that is all
    He gives me in reply.

Please tell me Katy's other name —
  I really want to know;
For should I find her much to blame,
  It would not vex me so.

To whom does this strange Kate belong?
  Is she your little wife?
And have you sung that noisy song
  Through all your married life?

And thus I question; but in vain,
  For in the darkness hid,
He utters not another strain
  But that shrill "Katy-did."
                — *Selected.*

TRUANT.

TOMMY thought there was nobody looking
  When he came running over the hill;
Stopping to hide in a thicket of willows,
  Till the bell in the village was still.

Tommy thought there was no one to see him,
  None in the road, or the fields, or the wood,
But all the willows, and all the grasses,
  And clouds and daisies could see where he stood.

All the buttercups standing together,
  All the wild roses that stood by the way,
Laughed and rustled, "See Tommy, see Tommy,
  Tommy played truant to-day."

Bees and butterflies flying before him,
  Told the story deep in the wood,
"Here comes Tommy, here comes Tommy,
  Tommy hasn't been good."

Saucy waves laughed out in the river,
  "Tommy had lessons to-day,
He's so careless, and lazy, and dull,
  He wanted to run away."

So all day wherever he wandered,
  So whatever he tried to do,
Everything was upbraiding Tommy.
  I think he deserved it. Don't you?
                  — *S. A. Hudson.*

LADYBIRD, LADYBIRD.

LADYBIRD, ladybird! fly away home!
  The field-mouse has gone to her nest,
The daisies have shut up their sleepy red eyes,
  And the bees and the birds are at rest.

Ladybird, ladybird! fly away home!
  The glow-worm is lighting her lamp,
The dew's falling fast, and your fine speckled wings
  Will flag with the close-clinging damp.

Ladybird, ladybird! fly away home!
  Good luck if you reach it at last!
The owl's come abroad, and the bat's on the roam,
  Sharp set from their Ramazan[1] fast.

[1] Ramazan, the holy month of the Mohammedans, in which they keep their lenten fast.

Ladybird, ladybird! fly away home!
  The fairy bells tinkle afar!
Make haste or they'll catch you, and harness you fast
  With a cobweb to Oberon's car.

Ladybird, ladybird! fly away home!
  To your house in the old willow-tree,
Where your children so dear have invited the ant
  And a few cozy neighbors to tea.

Ladybird, ladybird! fly away home!
  And if not gobbled up by the way,
Nor yoked by the fairies to Oberon's car,
  You're in luck! and that's all I've to say!
                    — *Caroline B. Southey.*

LADYBUG, LADYBUG.

LADYBUG, ladybug, haste away home!
  Your house is on fire,
Your children will burn.
    Dear ladybug, I am sorry for you
If your house is on fire.
    Oh, what will you do?

And your poor little children
  All burning, dear me!
It does seem as cruel
  As cruel can be.
Oh, why don't you hurry,
  You slow little elf?
If I knew where you lived,
  I would go there myself.

The house might burn down
　　While you're turning about.
'Tis because you are feeling
　　So badly, no doubt,
That you hardly can stir —
　　No wonder, poor dear!
You must be half crazy
　　Such bad news to hear;
Though I've told it to dozens,
I think, beside you, I feel
Just like crying whenever I do.
Now think of your babies!
　　Run, ladybug, run!
I do hope some neighbor
　　Has saved every one
From the terrible fire.
　　And ladybug, then,
You can build a new house,
　　And be happy again.
　　　　　　　　　　　　— *Selected.*

MRS. BRINDLE'S COWSLIP FEAST.

A COW lived in a pleasant field,
　　Where cowslips bloomed in spring.
Said she, "I think a cowslip feast
　　Would be a pleasant thing."

So Mrs. Brindle sent a calf
　　Around the farm, to say
That she should give a cowslip feast
　　At four o'clock that day.

At four o'clock she sat in state
  Beside the flowing brook;
The cowslips, with their golden heads,
  Did most inviting look.

The brindle calf in apron stood
  To ope the five-barred gate;
And then his mother said that he
  Upon the guests must wait.

The company at length drew near;
  First Mrs. Blossom came,
And Mrs. Dun, and Mr. Bull,
  Who seemed to-day quite tame.

Red, spotted, white, a goodly band
  Of cows and calves came nigh;
And Mr. Donkey said that he
  Would cowslips like to try.

And Mrs. Mare came with her foal,
  And Mr. Horse came too,
And several sheep with frisky lambs,
  In woolen dresses new.

Then Mrs. Brindle bade her guests
  The cowslips sweet to eat;
And if they wished to drink, she said,
  The brook was clear and sweet.

They ate and drank, and chatted too;
  And, when they went away,
Said, "Thank you, for your cowslip feast,
  Dear brindle cow, to-day."

—Selected.

THE OXEN.

THE oxen are such clever beasts,
    They'll drag the plow all day;
They're very strong, and tug along
    Great loads of wood or hay.

They feed on grass, when green or dry;
    Their flesh is beef, for food;
Their lungs are "lights," their stomach tripe,
    Their skin for leather's good.

Their hair men use in mortar too —
    Lime, water, sand, and hair,
They nicely mix and smoothly fix,
    For plastering, so fair.

For making soap their bones are used;
    Their horns for combs we group;
Their feet are boiled for "neat's-foot oil,"
    Their tails for ox-tail soup.

Their heart-case forms a money-bag;
    Their tallow, candles white;
Their intestine, gold-beater's skin,
    With each gold-leaf we smite.

Thus every part is useful made;
    The same is true of cows, —
Except their ilk gives luscious milk
    Instead of dragging plows.

Oxen and cows are "cattle" called;
    They go in "herds" when wild;
And when they're tame by other name, —
    A "drove," *en masse* they're styled.

Their little ones are "calves"—and cows'
  Rich milk produces cream,
Which butter makes, and nice cheese-cakes
  With curd, whey, and caseine.

And now 'tis funny, but 'tis true,
  Some children young and mazy,
Have thought their eyes were used some-wise
  To make the ox-eyed daisy.

This cannot be, yet creatures' bones
  Placed round trees, plants, and bowers
Will serve to feed just what they need,
  To grow fine fruits and flowers.
—*Selected.*

MRS. PUSSY.

MRS. PUSSY, sleek and fat,
  With her kittens four
Went to sleep upon the mat
  By the kitchen door.

Mrs. Pussy heard a noise,
  Up she jumped to see;
"Kittens, maybe that's a mouse,
  Let us go and see."

Creeping, creeping, creeping on,
  Silently they stole,
But that little mouse had gone
  Back into its hole.

"Well," said Mrs. Pussy, there,
  "To the barn we'll go;
We shall find the swallows there
  Flying to and fro."

So the cat and kittens four
  Tried their very best;
But the swallows flying fast
  Safely reached the nest.

Home went hungry Mrs. Puss
  And her kittens four;
Found their dinner on a plate,
  By the kitchen door.

As they gathered round the plate,
  They agreed 'twas nice
That it couldn't run away
  Like the birds and mice.
                                — *Selected.*

A BOY'S SONG.

WHERE the pools are bright and deep,
  Where the gray trout lies asleep,
Up the river and over the lea,
That's the way for Billy and me.

Where the blackbird sings the latest,
Where the hawthorn blooms the sweetest,
Where the nestlings chirp and flee,
That's the way for Billy and me.

Where the mowers mow the cleanest,
Where the hay lies thick and greenest,
There to trace the homeward bee,
That's the way for Billy and me.

Where the hazel bank is steepest,
Where the shadow falls the deepest,
Where the clustering nuts fall free,
That's the way for Billy and me.

Why the boys should drive away
Little sweet maidens from the play,
Or love to banter and fight so well,
That's the thing I never could tell.

But this I know, I love to play,
Through the meadow, among the hay;
Up the water and o'er the lea,
That's the way for Billy and me.

— *The Ettrick Shepherd*

THE COTTON PLANT.

SING, oh sing for the cotton plant!
   Bravely may it grow,
Bearing in its seeded pod
   Cotton white as snow!

Spin the cotton into thread;
   Weave it in the loom;
Wear it now, dear little child,
   In your happy home.

When you've worn it well and long,
    Will it worthless be?
No; a book made from this dress
    You yet, in time, may see.

Sort the rags and grind the pulp;
    Weave the paper fair;
Now it only waits for words
    To be printed there.

Thoughts from God to man sent down
    May these pages show.
Sing, oh sing for the cotton plant!
    Bravely may it grow!

May ten thousand cotton plants
    Spring up fresh and fair,
That words of wisdom and of love
    O'er all the world shall bear.

—Selected.

TWO OF A TRADE.

THE dragon-fly and I together
    Sail up the stream in the summer weather;
He at the stern, all green and gold,
And I at the oars, our course to hold.

Above the floor of the level river
The bent blades dip and spring and quiver;
And the dragon-fly is here and there,
Along the water and in the air.

And thus we go as the sunshine mellows,
A pair of nature's merriest fellows;
For the Spanish cedar is light and true,
And instead of one, it has carried two.

And thus we sail without care or sorrow,
With trust for to-day and hope for to-morrow;
He at the stern, all green and gold,
And I at the oars, our course to hold.
—*S. W. Duffield.*

A SUMMER LULLABY.

THE sun has gone from the shining skies;
    Bye, baby, bye,
The dandelions have closed their eyes;
    Bye, baby, bye.
And the stars are lighting their lamps to see
If the babies and squirrels and birds, all three,
Are sound asleep as they ought to be.
    Bye, baby, bye.

The squirrel is dressed in a coat of gray;
    Bye, baby, bye.
He wears it by night as well as by day;
    Bye, baby, bye.
The robin sleeps in his feathers and down,
With the warm red breast and the wings of brown;
But the baby wears a little white gown.
    Bye, baby, bye.

The squirrel's nest is a hole in the tree;
    Bye, baby, bye.
And there he sleeps as snug as can be;
    Bye, baby, bye.
The robin's nest is high overhead,
Where the leafy boughs of the maple spread,
But the baby's nest is a little white bed.
    Bye, baby, bye.

        — *E. S. Bumstead — St. Nicholas.*

THE SONG IN THE NIGHT.

A LITTLE bird sang in the dead of the night,
    When the moon peeped out through a cloud;
He sang, for his heart was so full of delight,
    It seemed almost throbbing aloud.

"Hush! hush!" cried the old birds; "you foolish young
    thing,
    To wake up and sing for the moon!
Come, tuck your silly head under your wing;
    You'll rouse our good neighbors too soon."

But the little bird flew to the top of the tree,
    And looked up into the sky.
"Our time for singing is short," quoth he,
    "And sing in the night will I."

        — *James Buckham — St. Nicholas.*

JAPANESE LULLABY.

SLEEP, little pigeon, and fold your wings, —
  Little blue pigeon with velvet eyes;
Sleep to the singing of mother-bird swinging —
  Swinging the nest where her little one lies.

Away out yonder I see a star, —
  Silvery star with a tinkling song;
To the soft dew falling I hear it calling —
  Calling and tinkling the night along.

In through the window a moonbeam comes, —
  Little gold moonbeam with misty wings;
All silently creeping, it asks, " Is he sleeping —
  Sleeping and dreaming while mother sings?"

Up from the sea there floats the sob
  Of the waves that are breaking upon the shore,
As though they were groaning in anguish, and moaning —
  Bemoaning the ship that shall come in no more.

But sleep, little pigeon, and fold your wings,
  Little blue pigeon with mournful eyes;
Am I not singing? — see, I am swinging —
  Swinging the nest where my darling lies.

— *Eugene Field — A Little Book of Western Verse.*

CRADLE SONG.

O BLUE eyes close in slumber;
   O birdie on your nest
Sing to my sleepless darling
   A little song of rest.

O wind among the roses,
   Soft through the window creep,
And with your murmur music
   Hush baby off to sleep.

O bee, that such soft wooing
   Makes for the lily's sake,
Come, sing your song of summer
   To little wide-awake.

O cricket on the hearthstone
   Chirp low, and soft, and long,
Till little, restless baby
   Grows drowsy with your song.

And whisper to my darling
   That mother's heart will keep
A watch o'er every movement
   While baby is asleep.

—*Caris Brooke.*

CHILDHOOD FANCIES.

THE twilight gray is falling;
   Now list and you shall hear
The footsteps of the sylphid fays,
   This is their hour of cheer.

List to the gentle patter
   On each wee blade of grass,
As it is bent, and back again,
   Whene'er the fairies pass.

Upon the tips of grasses
   They cross the meadow lawn,
And laugh and dance and play and sing,
   From twilight hour till dawn.

They light their myriad lanterns,
   And hang them in the arch
Of blue that canopies o'erhead,
   And by their light they march.

They sometimes miss a fairy,
   And take a lantern down
To search for her, and mortals say:
   "A firefly flits around."

On leaves they hang their diamonds,
   Their pearls in every flower;
Their gauzy veils upon the grass
   They spread for fairy bower.

Their slender wings are hanging
  On every shrub, across;
Their seats are dainty cushion-beds
  Of green and springy moss.

Their shrubbery of coral
  Is gray and scarlet-tipped;
Their hair upon the maize is hung
  Each summer, when 'tis clipped.

The mushroom forms their table,
  Their dishes, acorn cups;
The ant-hills are their barracks high;
  Their cannon, "hemlock pops."

Their scarfs of plush are lying
  On ripening grape and peach;
Their sea-shells 'neath the apple-trees,
  Each spring bestrews their beach.

They paint the leaves in autumn;
  They make a tiny rink
Of every puddle, fen, and dike,
  And skate from wave to brink.

They brown the nuts in forests,
  The burrs they open wide;
They lure the feathers from the clouds,
  And pile them up, to slide.

They build along the wayside
  Their fairy palisades, —
The "hoar-frost" some have christened it, —
  And hold West Point parades.

They sketch upon the windows
　Such pictures as no power
Of man can ever execute,
　And on them pearl-dust shower.

All these, and myriad fancies
　That never can be told,
My childhood days so new and sweet,
　In memory infold.

But mother softly whispers,
　"'Tis not the fays, my dears,
'Tis old Dame Nature's song of songs,
　The 'Music of the Spheres.'

"List ever for it, children,
　'Twill bring you close to God!
Each sound but echoes Him who made,
　Each motion is His nod."
　　　　　　　　— *Mother Truth's Melodies.*

SONGS OF AUTUMN.

Songs of Autumn.

THE SEASONS.

FOUR babies lay in their cradles new,
Beginning to think of "What shall I do
The world to brighten and beautify?"
The Spring baby first said, "Let me try."

So she put on a dress of freshest green,
With trimmings the loveliest ever seen —
Trimmings of tulips and hyacinths rare
And trailing arbutus looped everywhere.

"How perfectly beautiful!" Summer said;
"But wait till you see my dress of red
And darker green with golden spots,
Trimmed with roses and pinks and forget-me-nots."

"Pooh!" said Autumn, "my dress will be
A more substantial one, you'll see;
With skirt of finest and yellowest wheat,
A girdle of grapes and squash turban neat."

Then Winter came silently tripping along,
Chanting softly a Christmas song,
In a pure white dress with jewels spread,
Holding a basket of books on his head.

Poems and stories and pictures were there
Of the Christ child, the Yule log of folk-lore rare.
"I am not in bright colors," he said, with a smile,
"But the long winter evenings my gifts here beguile."
— *Helen Adelaide Ricker.*

LOST: THE SUMMER.

WHERE has the summer gone?
    She was here just a minute ago,
With roses and daisies
To whisper her praises —
And every one loved her so!

Has any one seen her about?
    She must have gone off in the night!
      And she took the best flowers
      And the happiest hours,
And asked no one's leave for her flight.

Have you noticed her steps in the grass?
    The garden looks red where she went;
      By the side of the hedge
      There's a goldenrod edge,
And the rose-vines are withered and bent.

Don't you fear she is sorry she went?
    It seems but a minute since May!
      I'm scarcely half through
      What I wanted to do;
If she only had waited a day!

Do you think she will ever come back?
I shall watch every day at the gate
  For the robins and clover,
  Saying over and over:
"I know she will come, if I wait!"
      —*R. M. Alden — The Pansy, Sept.*, 1894.

AUTUMN.

THE world puts on its robes of glory now;
  The very flowers are tinged with deeper dyes;
The waves are bluer, and the angels pitch
  Their shining tents along the sunset skies.

The distant hills are crowned with purple mist;
  The days are mellow, and the long calm nights,
To wondering eyes, like weird magicians show
  The shifting splendors of the Northern Lights.

The generous earth spreads out her faithful stores,
  And all the leaves are thick with ripened sheaves;
While in the woods, at Autumn's rustling step,
  The maples blush through all their trembling leaves.
      —*Albert Laighton*.

AUTUMN SONG.

NO clouds are in the morning sky
  The vapors hug the stream —
Who says that life and love can die
  In all this northern gleam!

At every turn the maples burn,
  The quail is whistling free,
The partridge whirrs, and the frosted burrs
  Are dropping for you and me.
    Ho! hilly ho! heigh O!
      Hilly ho!
In the clear October morning.

Along our path the woods are bold
  And glow with ripe desire;
The yellow chestnut showers its gold,
  The sumachs spread their fire;
The breezes feel as crisp as steel,
  The buckwheat tops are red:
Then down the lane, love, scurry again,
  And over the stubble tread!
    Ho! hilly ho! heigh O!
      Hilly ho!
In the clear October morning.
                    — *E. C. Stedman.*

ABOUT THE FAIRIES.

PRAY, where are the little bluebells gone,
  That lately bloomed in the wood?
Why, the little fairies have each taken one,
  And put it on for a hood.

And where are the pretty grass-stalks gone,
  That waved in the summer breeze?
Oh, the fairies have taken them every one,
  To plant in their gardens, like trees.

And where are the great big bluebottles gone,
  That buzzed in their busy pride?
Oh, the fairies have caught them every one,
  And have broken them in to ride.

And they've taken the glow-worms to light their halls,
  And the cricket to sing them a song,
And the great red rose-leaves to paper their walls,
  And they're feasting the whole night long.

But when spring comes, with its soft, mild ray,
  And the ripple of gentle rain,
The fairies bring back what they've taken away,
  And give it us all again.
— *Selected.*

TRIFLES.

A RAINDROP is a little thing,
  But on the thirsty ground,
It helps to make the flowers of spring,
  And beauty spread around.

A ray of light may seem to be
  Lost in the blaze of day;
But its sweet mission God can see,
  Who sends it on its way.
— *Colesworthy.*

SUNSHINE.

I WISH the beautiful sun would shine,
    Every, every day,
Beaming over the whole great world,
    And making it bright and gay.

I wish that every gloomy cloud
    Would hurry and hide away,
Wherever it came from — I don't know
    Nor care — if they'd go and stay.

I wish, I wish — but what is the use
    Of wishing, I'd like to know?
For grandmother says that clouds and shine
    Will always come and go.

But wee little girls like me, she says,
    Can smile, and smile, and smile,
Till every one who sees will think
    It is sunshine all the while.

I'd like to try it, but, don't you see,
    A bit of a smile like mine
Would reach such a very little way
    And make such a little shine?

But ah — if every boy and girl
    Would smile, and smile, and see
How far they could make the brightness go,
    How shining the world would be!

—Selected.

SEPTEMBER.

THE goldenrod is yellow;
   The corn is turning brown;
The trees in apple orchards
   With fruit are bending down.

The gentian's bluest fringes
   Are curling in the sun;
In dusty pools the milkweed
   Its hidden silk has spun.

The sedges flaunt their harvest,
   In every meadow nook;
And asters by the brook-side
   Make asters in the brook.

From dewy lanes at morning
   The grapes' sweet odors rise;
At noon the roads all flutter
   With yellow butterflies.

By all these lovely tokens
   September days are here,
With summer's best of weather,
   And autumn's best of cheer.
               — *Helen Hunt Jackson.*

GOLDENROD.

TELL me, sunny goldenrod,
   Growing everywhere,
Did fairies come from fairyland
   And make the dress you wear?

Did you get from mines of gold
  Your bright and shining hue?
Or did the baby stars some night
  Fall down and cover you?

Or did the angels wave their wings
  And drop their glitter down
Upon you, laughing goldenrod,
  Your nodding head to crown?

Or are you clad in sunshine
  Caught from summer's brightest day,
To give again in happy smiles
  To all who pass your way?

I love you, laughing goldenrod,
  And I will try, like you,
To fill each day with deeds of cheer;
  Be loving, kind, and true.
                            —*Mrs. F. J. Lovejoy.*

GOLDENROD.

"How in the world did I happen to bloom
  All by myself, alone
By the side of a dusty country road,
  With only a rough old stone

"For company?" And the golden-rod,
  As she drooped her yellow head,
Gave a mournful sigh. "Who cares for me,
  Or knows I'm alive?" she said.

"A snow-white daisy I'd like to be,
  Half hid in the cool green sod;
Or a pink spiræa, or a sweet wild rose —
  But I'm *only a goldenrod!*

"Nobody knows that I'm here, nor cares
  Whether I live or die!
Lovers of beautiful flowers, who wants
  Such a common thing as I?"

But all of a sudden she ceased her plaint;
  For a child's voice cried in glee,
"Here's a dear, little, lovely goldenrod!
  Did you bloom on purpose for me?

"Down by the brook the tall spiræa
  And the purple asters nod,
And beckon to me — but more than all
  Do I love *you*, goldenrod!"

She raised the flower to her rosy lips,
  And merrily kissed its face.
"Ah! now I see," said the goldenrod,
  "How this is the very place

"That was meant for me; and I'm glad I bloomed
  Just here by the road alone,
With nobody near for company
  But a dear old mossy stone!"

— *Selected.*

IN SEPTEMBER.

MORNINGS frosty grow, and cold,
Brown the grass on hill and wold;
Crows are cawing sharp and clear
When the rustling corn grows sere;
Mustering flocks of blackbirds call,
Here and there a few leaves fall,
In the meadows larks sing sweet,
Chirps the cricket at our feet,
     In September.

Noons are sunny, warm, and still,
A golden haze o'erhangs the hill,
Amber sunshine's on the floor
Just within the open door.
Still the crickets call and creak,
Never found, though long we seek;
Oft comes faint report of gun,
Busy flies buzz in the sun,
     In September.

Evenings chilly are, and damp,
Early lighted is the lamp;
Fire burns, and kettle sings,
Smoke ascends in thin blue rings;
On the rug the children lie,
In the west the soft lights die,
From the elms a robin's song
Rings out sweetly, lingers long,
     In September.

—Sunday Afternoon.

THE SPIRIT OF THE SUNSET.

WHEN the aster wakes in the morning,
   In these sweet autumn days,
She sees the sumach burning,
   And the maples in a blaze,
And she rubs her eyes, bewildered,
   All in the golden haze.
Then: "No, — they still are standing;
   They're not on fire at all" —
She softly says, when slowly
   She sees some crimson fall,
And yellow flakes come floating
   Down from the oaks so tall.
And then she knows the spirit
   Of the sunset must have planned
The myriad bright surprises
   That deck the dying land, —
And she wonders if the sumach
   And the maples understand.

— Selected.

GENTIAN.

IN spring I found the violet
   And rosy Mayflowers sweet;
And next, white-fingered daisy
   Was courtesying at my feet;

Then wild rose swung her censer,
   And, in a secret hour,
The lonely meadow flamed abroad
   With gorgeous cardinal flower.

Soon goldenrod close followed
   And aster's gentle eye;
Now withered leaves and dying sod
   Beneath a somber sky.

I start — among the grasses
   What eyes of heaven-blue gleam,
All darkly fringed with lashes
   Beside the quiet stream?

Oh! glance of true affection,
   The gentian still is here;
The promise set 'mid fading,
   The darling of the year.

—*Kate L. Brown.*

MARIGOLDS.

Dame Nature years and years ago
   Sat resting in a wayside bower,
And looked into a cottage yard
Without the grace of one wee flower,
To thank for light the sweet blue skies,
And bless the children's longing eyes.

She leaned her head upon her hand,
And took her glasses off to think;
"Sunshine there is to spare," she said,
"And dew enough for all to drink,
If there were many blossoms more
To grow upon the earth's green floor."

Then rising quickly from her seat
She plucked beneath the cottage eaves
The sunbeams that were wasted there,
And bound them into tiny sheaves,
Tied them with dainty bands of green,
And then, on tall stems scarcely seen,

Set them beside the cottage door,
Beneath the wall, and by the gate,
And when the morning came that way
It found them all in golden state:
Gay blossoms lifted toward the sky,
And nodding to a butterfly.

The dew was on their shining heads
Just ruffled by the laughing breeze;
The children danced and clapped their hands;
Out from the corn-flowers flew the bees;
All summer breathed in their rich folds,
And people called them marigolds.
—*Susan Hartley.*

THE FLAX FLOWER.

OH, the little flax flower!
   It groweth on the hill,
And, be the breeze awake or 'sleep,
   It never standeth still.
It groweth, and it groweth fast;
   One day it is a seed,

And then a little grassy blade
   Scarce better than a weed.
But then out comes the flax flower
   As blue as is the sky;
And "'Tis a dainty little thing,"
   We say as we go by.

Ah! 'tis a goodly little thing;
   It groweth for the poor,
And many a peasant blesseth it
   Beside his cottage door.
He thinketh how those slender stems
   That shimmer in the sun,
Are rich for him in web or woof
   And shortly shall be spun.
He thinketh how those tender flowers
   Of seed will yield him store,
And sees in thought his next year's crop,
   Blue shining round his door.

Oh, the little flax flower!
   The mother then says she,
"Go, pull the thyme, the heath, the fern,
   But let the flax flower be!
It groweth for the children's sake,
   It groweth for our own;
There are flowers enough upon the hill,
   But leave the flax alone!
The farmer hath his fields of wheat,
   Much cometh to his share;
We have this little plot of flax,
   That we have tilled with care."

Oh, the goodly flax flower!
   It groweth on the hill,
And, be the breeze awake or 'sleep,
   It never standeth still;
It seemeth all astir with life,
   As if it loved to thrive,
As if it had a merry heart
   Within its stem alive.
Then fair befall the flax field,
   And may the kindly shower
Give strength unto its shining stem,
   Give seed unto its flower!
                        —*Mary Howitt.*

THE WIND.

"WHAT is the wind, mamma?"
   "'Tis air in motion, child."
"Why can I never see the wind
   That blows so fierce and wild?"

"Because the gases, dear,
   Of which the air is made,
Are quite transparent; that is, we
   See through, but see no shade."

"And what are gases, ma?"
   "Fluids, which, if we squeeze
In space too small, will burst with force."
   "And what are fluids, please?"

"Fluids are what will flow,
  And gases are so light
That, when we give them room enough,
  They rush with eager flight."

"What gases, dear mamma,
  Make up the air or wind?"
"'Tis oxygen and nitrogen
  That chiefly there we find;

"And when the air is full
  Of oxygen, we're gay,
But when there is not quite enough,
  We're dull or faint away."
— *Mother Truth's Melodies.*

THE POINTS OF THE COMPASS.

SAID Wind to the bright little weather vane,
  "I'll teach you, I'll teach you;
Mind my commands, come sunshine or rain;
  I'll teach you, I'll teach you."

Said Wind to the bright little weather vane,
  "Find east, dear, the east, dear,
'Tis where the sun comes up again;
  The east, dear, the east, dear.

"Now turn to the west where the sun goes down,
  The west, dear, the west, dear,
See all the little clouds wear a shining crown,
  In the west, dear, in the west, dear.

"Now turn to the south, where the warm winds blow,
  The south, dear, the south, dear.
You will like that best of all, I know,
  The south, dear, the south, dear.

"Now turn to the home of the north wind bold,
  Find north, dear, the north, dear,
Ugh! ice and snow — but who cares for the cold?
  The north, dear, the north, dear.

"North, west, east, and south, now find in turn;
  That's right, dear, just right, dear,
You're a brave little fellow and quick to learn;
  Good-night, dear, good-night, dear."

— *Selected.*

AUTUMN LEAVES.

"Come, little leaves," said the wind one day,
  "Come over the meadows with me, and play;
Put on your dresses of red and gold;
Summer is gone, and the days grow cold."

Soon as the leaves heard the wind's loud call,
Down they came fluttering, one and all;
Over the brown fields they danced and flew,
Singing the soft little songs they knew.

"Cricket, good-bye, we've been friends so long;
Little brook, sing us your farewell song —
Say you're sorry to see us go;
Ah! you are sorry, right well we know.

"Dear little lambs, in your fleecy fold,
Mother will keep you from harm and cold;
Fondly we've watched you in vale and glade;
Say, will you dream of our loving shade?"

Dancing and whirling the little leaves went;
Winter had called them and they were content—
Soon fast asleep in their earthy beds,
The snow laid a soft mantle over their heads.
—Selected.

THE LITTLE LEAVES.

"We must go," sighed little Ruby,
    Orange, Topaz, Garnet, Gold;
"For the chilly breeze is calling,
    And the year is growing old.
Good-bye, quiet, sunny meadow,
    That we nevermore shall see;
Good-bye, winding brooks of silver,
    Snow lambs and dear old tree —
    Dear old loving mother tree."

From the branches down they fluttered
    Like a rainbow scattered wide;
And the old tree looked so lonely,
    That was once the woodland's pride;
But the wind came wildly piping,
    And they danced in glee;
Ruby, Topaz, Garnet, Orange,
    Soon forgot the poor old tree —
    Poor old loving mother tree.

But when skies of drear November
   Frowned upon their wild delight,
All the little leaves grew lonely,
   And they wandered back one night,
And they nestled in a hollow
   At the foot of the old tree,
Sighing, "All the long white winter
   We shall now as quiet be,
   Near our dear old mother tree."

                  — *George Cooper.*

HOW THE LEAVES CAME DOWN.

"I'LL tell you how the leaves came down."
   The great tree to his children said,
"You're getting sleepy, Yellow and Brown,
   Yes, very sleepy, little Red.
   It is quite time to go to bed."

"Ah!" begged each silly, pouting leaf,
   "Let us a little longer stay;
Dear Father Tree, behold our grief;
   'Tis such a very pleasant day
   We do not want to go away."

So, for just one more merry day
   To the great tree the leaflets clung,
Frolicked and danced, and had their way,
   Upon the autumn breezes swung,
   Whispering all their sports among, —

"Perhaps the great tree will forget,
  And let us stay until the spring,
If we all beg, and coax, and fret."
  But the great tree did no such thing;
  He smiled to hear their whispering.

"Come, children, all to bed," he cried;
  And ere the leaves could urge their prayer,
He shook his head, and far and wide,
  Fluttering and rustling everywhere,
  Down sped the leaflets through the air.

I saw them; on the ground they lay,
  Golden and red, a huddled swarm,
Waiting till one from far away,
  White bedclothes heaped upon her arm,
  Should come to wrap them safe and warm.

The great bare tree looked down and smiled,
  "Good-night, dear little leaves," he said.
And from below each sleepy child
  Replied, "Good-night," and murmurèd,
  "It is so nice to go to bed!"
                —*Susan Coolidge.*

OCTOBER'S BRIGHT BLUE WEATHER.

SUN and skies and clouds of June,
  And flowers of June together,
Ye cannot rival for one hour
  October's bright blue weather;

When loud the bumblebee makes haste,
   Belated, thriftless vagrant,
And goldenrod is dying fast,
   And lanes with grapes are fragrant;

When gentians roll their fingers tight
   To save them for the morning,
And chestnuts fall from satin burrs
   Without a sound of warning;

When on the ground red apples lie
   In piles like jewels shining,
And redder still on old stone walls
   Are leaves of woodbine twining;

When all the lovely wayside things
   Their white-winged seeds are sowing,
And in the fields, still green and fair,
   Late aftermaths are growing;

When springs run low, and on the brooks,
   In idle golden freighting,
Bright leaves sink noiseless in the hush
   Of woods, for winter waiting;

When comrades seek sweet country haunts,
   By twos and twos together,
And count like misers, hour by hour,
   October's bright blue weather.

O sun and skies and flowers of June,
   Count all your boasts together,
Love loveth best of all the year
   October's bright blue weather.

              —*Helen Hunt Jackson.*

OCTOBER'S PARTY.

OCTOBER gave a party;
    The leaves by hundreds came,
The Chestnuts, Oaks, and Maples,
    And leaves of every name.

The sunshine spread a carpet,
    And everything was grand;
Miss Weather led the dancing,
    Professor Wind the band.

The Chestnuts came in yellow,
    The Oaks in crimson dressed,
The lovely Misses Maple
    In scarlet looked their best.

All balanced to their partners
    And gaily fluttered by;
The sight was like a rainbow
    New fallen from the sky.

Then in the rustic hollow
    At hide-and-seek they played;
The party closed at sundown
    And everybody stayed.

Professor Wind played louder;
    They flew along the ground,
And then the party ended
    In hands across, all round.

—Song Stories for Little Folk.

LITTLE BY LITTLE.

WHILE the new years come, and the old years go,
   How, little by little, all things grow!
All things grow, and all decay —
Little by little passing away.
Little by little, on fertile plain,
Ripen the harvests of golden grain,
Waving and flashing in the sun
When the summer at last is done.

Low on the ground an acorn lies —
Little by little it mounts the skies,
Shadow and shelter for wandering herds,
Home for a hundred singing birds.
Little by little the great rocks grew,
Long, long ago, when the world was new;
Slowly and silently, stately and free,
Cities of coral under the sea
Little by little are builded, while so
The new years come and the old years go.

Little by little all tasks are done;
So are the crowns of the faithful won,
So is heaven in our hearts begun.
With work and with weeping, with laughter and play,
Little by little, the longest day
And the longest life are passing away —
Passing without return, while so
The new years come and the old years go.

—Selected.

A CHANCE.

"Give me a chance," an acorn said,
  "And I'll grow to a mighty tree,
And then, perchance, on a summer's day,
  In my shadow I'll shelter thee."

"Give me a chance," said the rose-bush small,
  "And I'll bloom with a beauty rare,
And out of my heart in its gratitude
  For you I will scent the air."

"Give me a chance," said a bobolink,
  "And I'll sing you a merry song,
That will throb in your heart like a bit of heaven
  Throughout your whole life long."

"Give me a chance," said a little child,
  "And I'll touch that heart of thine,
And thou wilt feel as once thou felt
  When the world was all divine."
—Selected.

THE CHESTNUT BURR

A WEE little nut lay deep in its nest
  Of satin and brown, the softest and best,
And slept and grew while its cradle rocked,
As it hung in the boughs that interlocked.

Now the house was small where the cradle lay,
As it swung in the winds by night and day;
For a thicket of underbrush fenced it round,
This lone little cot, by the great sun browned.

This little nut grew, and erelong it found
There was work outside on the soft green ground;
It must do its part, so the world might know
It had tried one little seed to sow.

And soon the house that had kept it warm
Was tossed about by the autumn storm,
The stem was cracked, the old house fell,
And the chestnut burr was an empty shell.

But the little tree, as it waiting lay,
Dreamed a wonderful dream one day,
Of how it should break its coat of brown,
And live as a tree, to grow up and down.
—*Selected.*

NUTTING.

COME, Robert and Harry, come, Lily and May!
October is here, and our glad holiday.
With every breath of the keen, frosty breeze,
Brown chestnuts are dropping from all the high trees.

Come here with your bags and your big baskets, quick,
And Harry's new jack-knife shall cut a long stick.
Then Robert shall climb the old chestnut-tree tall,
And thrash the big boughs till the ripe chestnuts fall.

So shiny and smooth, and so plump and so brown,
The handsomest chestnuts that ever fell down;
Though stately and proud the old nut tree has stood
A hundred long years — the king of the wood.

You dear little squirrel, you look very wise,
With long bushy tail and bright, shiny, black eyes.
Pray, sir, do you fancy you own the big tree?
It's quite a mistake, sir, between you and me.

We don't mean to rob you, dear, not in the least,
But we too like chestnuts, and long for a feast;
We know you must gather your snug winter store,
But after we go you will find plenty more.
— *Selected.*

LITTLE NUT PEOPLE.

OLD Mistress Chestnut once lived in a burr,
Padded and lined with the softest of fur.
Jack Frost split it wide with his keen silver knife,
And tumbled her out at the risk of her life.

Here is Don Almond, a grandee from Spain,
Some raisins from Malaga came in his train;
He has a twin brother a shade or two leaner,
When both come together we shout "Philopena!"

This is Sir Walnut; he's English, you know,
A friend of my Lady and Lord So-and-So.
Whenever you ask old Sir Walnut to dinner,
Be sure and have wine for the gouty old sinner.

Little Miss Peanut, from North Carolina,
She's not 'ristocratic but no nut is finer.
Sometimes she is roasted and burnt to a cinder,
In Georgia they call her Miss Goober, or Pinder.

Little Miss Hazelnut, in her best bonnet,
Is lovely enough to be put in a sonnet;
And young Mr. Filbert has journeyed from Kent,
To ask her to marry him soon after Lent.

This is old Hickory; look at him well,
A general was named for him, so I've heard tell.
Take care how you hit him. He sometimes hits back!
This stolid old chap is a hard nut to crack.

Old Mr. Butternut just from Brazil,
Is rugged and rough as the side of a hill;
But, like many a countenance quite as ill-favored,
His covers a kernel deliciously flavored.

Here is a Southerner, graceful and slim,
In flavor no nut is quite equal to him.
Ha, Monsieur Pecan, you know what it means,
To be served with black coffee in French New Orleans.

Dear little Chinquapin, modest and neat,
Isn't she cunning and isn't she sweet?
Her skin is as smooth as a little boy's chin,
And the squirrels all chatter of Miss Chinquapin.

And now, my dear children, I'm sure I have told
All the queer rhymes that a nutshell can hold.

— *E. J. Nicholson — St. Nicholas.*

THE GOSSIP OF THE NUTS.

SAID the Shagbark to the Chestnut,
   "Is it time to leave the burr?"
"I don't know," replied the Chestnut,
   "There's Hazelnut—ask her.

"I don't dare to pop my nose out,
   Till Jack Frost unlocks the door,
Besides, I'm in no hurry
   To increase the squirrels' store.

"A telegram from Peanut says
   That she is on the way;
And the Pecan Nuts are ripening,
   In Texas, so they say."

Just here the little Beechnut,
   In his three-cornered hat,
Remarked in tiny piping voice:
   "I'm glad to hear of that;

"For then my charming cousin
   So very much like me,
Miss Chinquapin will come with them,
   And happy I shall be."

Then Butternut spoke up and said:
   "'Twill not be long before
I'll have to move my quarters
   To the farmer's garret floor;

"With Hickory and Walnut,
   Good company I'll keep,
And there, until Thanksgiving,
   Together we shall sleep."

Said the Shagbark: "I am tired
   Of being cooped up here;
I want to go to see the world;
   Pray, what is there to fear?

"I'll stay up here no longer;
   I'll just go pouncing down.
So good-bye, Sister Chestnut!
   We'll meet again in town."

—*Selected.*

THE SQUIRREL'S ARITHMETIC.

HIGH on the branch of a walnut-tree
   A bright-eyed squirrel sat.
What was he thinking so earnestly?
   And what was he looking at?

The forest was green around him,
   The sky all over his head;
His nest was in a hollow limb,
   And his children snug in bed.

He was doing a problem o'er and o'er,
   Busily thinking was he;
How many nuts for this winter's store
   Could he hide in the hollow tree?

He sat so still on the swaying bough
   You might have thought him asleep.
Oh, no; he was trying to reckon now
   The nuts the babies could eat.

Then suddenly he frisked about,
   And down the tree he ran.
"The best way to do, without a doubt,
   Is to gather all I can."

—Selected.

TIME ENOUGH.

TWO little squirrels out in the sun,
   One gathered nuts, the other had none;
"Time enough yet," his constant refrain,
"Summer is only just on the wane."

Listen, my child, while I tell you his fate:
He roused him at last, but he roused him too late;
Down fell the snow from the pitiless cloud,
And gave little squirrel a spotless white shroud.

Two little boys in a school-room were placed,
One always perfect, the other disgraced;
"Time enough yet for my learning," he said,
"I'll climb by and by from the foot to the head."

Listen, my darling: Their locks have turned gray,
One as a governor is sitting to-day;
The other, a pauper, looks out at the door
Of the almshouse, and idles his days as of yore.

Two kinds of people we meet every day;
One is at work, the other at play, —
Living uncared for, dying unknown —
The business hive hath ever a drone.

Tell me, my child, if the squirrels have taught
The lesson I long to impart in your thought;
Answer me this, and my story is done,
Which of the two would you be, little one?
— *Selected.*

PLANT SONG.

"O WHERE do you come from, berries red,
 Nuts, apples and plums, that hang ripe overhead,
Sweet, juicy grapes, with your rich purple hue,
Saying, 'Pick us, and eat us; we're growing for you?'

"O where do you come from, bright flowers and fair,
That please with your colors and fragrance so rare,
Glowing in sunshine, or sparkling with dew?"
"We are blooming for dear little children like you;

"Our roots are our mouths, taking food from the ground,
Our leaves are our lungs, breathing air all around,
Our sap, like your blood, our veins courses through,
Don't you think, little children, we're somewhat like you?

"Your hearts are the soil, your thoughts are the seeds;
Your lives may become useful plants or foul weeds;
If you think but good thoughts, your lives will be true,
For good women and men were once children like you."
— *Nellie M. Brown.*

HITHER, MEADOW GOSSIP, TELL ME!

(TO A BEE.)

HITHER, meadow gossip, tell me,
   Will you never pause to rest?
From the gray of dawn I've watched you,
   Till the sun has burned the west;
Seen you whisper to the gentian
   What you heard upon the wheat;
And the flowers nod in laughter
   At the stories you repeat.

Long and vainly have I listened
   To discover what you said,
What you murmured to the daisies,
   To the clovers white and red;
And I saw you, after prowling
   Where the columbines were hid,
Set the apple blossoms blushing —
   Yes, you shocking wretch, you did!

Buttercups and dandelions
   Show you yellow heaps of gold,
Just to hearken to your chatter
   And the scandals you unfold;
Even Jack within his pulpit,
   Priestly rascal, likes to hear
Things about his congregation
   That should hurt a saintly ear.

And lest any of your items
   Through the day should be forgot,
I believe you always write them
   On the dim forget-me-not.

If I trust you with a secret
   Far more precious, little bee,
Will you tell me on the morrow
   If my sweetheart thinks of me!

Gentle tattler, I must love you,
   Though you have a meddling way;
And I would that human gossips
   Had the wisdom you display,
And could, leaving all their slanders
   And the meanness they must meet,
Journey homeward in the gloaming
   Bringing only what is sweet.
       —*H. Prescott Beach*—*New England Magazine.*

MAUDE AND THE CRICKET.

"GOOD-NIGHT, dear Maudie," I softly said,
   And tucked her in her little bed.
"Good-night, mamma," she said to me,
"I am just as sleepy as I can be."

But scarcely closed was the chamber door,
When her eager voice called out once more:
"Mamma," she said, "what is it I hear—
That strange little noise, so sharp and queer?"

I listened,—then told her all was still,
Save a merry cricket piping shrill;
"He is hidden in the closet here,
To sing you to sleep, my Maudie dear."

Then Maudie sat up in her night-dress white,
And her eyes grew big and round and bright.
"Now, dear mamma, please move my bed
Close up to the closet door," she said.

"Poor little fellow! He wants to speak.
And all he can say is 'Creak, creak, creak!'
I wish to tell him I hear his song,
And ask him to sing it all night long."

"I'll leave the door open," I said, "part way,
So the cricket can hear whatever you say;
Now, while I go to your baby brother,
You little crickets may sing to each other."

When soon again I crept up the stair,
And stood for a moment listening there,
Over the household was silence deep —
Maud and the cricket were both asleep.

When "sleepy time" came for Maude next night,
She rushed around like a fairy white;
Peeped into the closet and over the floor,
To find the little cricket once more.

He was not to be seen in any place,
So Maude lay down with a mournful face;
When under her crib a voice piped clear —
"Creak, creakety, creak! I'm here, I'm here!"

Then Maudie screamed with surprised delight;
And she always believed from that very night,
That crickets can hear when little girls speak,
And mean a great deal by their "Creak, creak, creak!"

— *Selected.*

THE CRICKET.

Little inmate, full of mirth,
  Chirping on my kitchen hearth,
Wheresoe'er be thine abode,
Always harbinger of good,
Pay me for thy warm retreat
With a song more soft and sweet;
In return thou shalt receive
Such a strain as I can give.

Neither night nor dawn of day
Puts a period to thy play!
Sing then and extend thy span
Far beyond the date of man.
Wretched man, whose years are spent
In repining discontent,
Lives not, aged though he be,
Half a span, compared with thee.
— *William Cowper.*

THE FROG'S GOOD-BYE.

Good-bye, little children, I'm going away,
  In my snug little home all winter to stay.
I seldom get up, once I'm tucked in my bed,
And as it grows colder I cover my head.

I sleep very quietly all winter through,
And really enjoy it; there's nothing to do,
The flies are all gone, so there's nothing to eat,
And I take this time to enjoy a good sleep.

My bed is a nice little hole in the ground,
Where snug as a bug in the winter I'm found.
You might think long fasting would make me grow thin,
But no! I stay plump as when I go in.

And now, little children, good-bye, one and all,
Some warm day next spring I shall give you a call;
I'm quite sure to know when to get out of bed, —
When I feel the warm sun shining down on my head.
—*Selected.*

THE SHINING WEB.

A HUNGRY spider made a web
   Of thread so very fine,
Your tiny fingers scarce could feel
   The little slender line.
      Round about and round about,
         And round about it spun;
      Straight across and back again,
         Until the web was done.

O what a pretty, shining web
   It was when it was done!
The little flies all came to see
   It hanging in the sun.
      Round about and round about,
         And round about they danced;
      Across the web and back again,
         They darted and they glanced.

The hungry spider sat and watched
  The happy little flies;
It saw all round about its head —
  It had so many eyes.
    Round about and round about,
      And round about they go;
    Across the web and back again,
      Now high again, now low.

"I am hungry, very hungry,"
  Said the spider to the fly;
"If you would come into my house,
  We'd eat some, you and I."
    But round about and round about,
      And round about once more;
    Across the web and back again,
      They flitted as before.

For all the flies were much too wise
  To venture near the spider;
They flapped their little wings and flew
  In circles rather wider.
    Round about and round about,
      And round about went they;
    Across the web and back again,
      And then they flew away.
          —*Selected.*

THE WANDERINGS OF THE BIRDS.

AUTUMN has come, so bare and gray,
  The woods are brown and red,
The flowers all have passed away,
  The forest leaves are dead.

The little birds at morning dawn,
   Clothed in warm coats of feather,
Conclude that they away will roam,
   To seek for milder weather.

The robin gives his last sweet strain,
   His mate responding, follows;
And then away they lead the train
   Of bluebirds, wrens, and swallows.

The cuckoo, thrush, and yellowbird,
   The wild goose, teal, and sparrow,
Martin, and chippy, all are heard
   To sing their parting carol.

The oriole hastens in his flight,
   The swallow skims the water;
The whip-poor-will and bobby white
   Join in the blackbirds' chatter.

Tribe after tribe with leaders fair,
   All spread their wings for flight.
Away, away, high in the air;
   Nor care for day and night.

The fig-tree and the orange bowers,
   They soon will find so sweet;
The sunny clime of fruits and flowers
   They with warm hearts will greet.

But when the voice of spring they hear,
   They'll sing their "chick-a-dee,"
And back they'll come our hearts to cheer,
   "Tu-whit, tu-whit, tu-whee."

—Songs for Little Ones at Home.

THE SPARROW'S NEST.

NAY, only look what I have found!
A sparrow's nest upon the ground;
A sparrow's nest, as you may see,
Blown out of yonder old elm-tree.

And what a medley thing it is!
I never saw a nest like this,
So neatly wove with decent care,
Of silvery moss and shining hair.

But put together, odds and ends,
Picked up from enemies and friends;
See, bits of thread, and bits of rag,
Just like a little rubbish bag!

See, hair of dog and fur of cat,
And rovings of a worsted mat,
And shreds of silks, and many a feather
Compacted cunningly together.

Well, here has hoarding been and living,
And not a little good contriving,
Before a home of peace and ease
Was fashioned out of things like these!

Think, had these odds and ends been brought
To some wise man renowned for thought,
Some man, of men the very gem,
Pray, what could he have done with them?

If we had said: " Here, sir, we bring
You many a worthless little thing,
Just bits and scraps, so very small
That they have scarcely size at all;

And out of these, you must contrive
A dwelling large enough for five;
Neat, warm, and snug; with comfort stored;
Where five small things may lodge and board.'

How would the man of learning vast
Have been astonished and aghast,
And vowed that such a thing had been
Ne'er heard of, thought of, much less seen!

Ah! man of learning, you are wrong;
Instinct is, more than wisdom, strong;
And He who made the sparrow, taught
This skill beyond your reach of thought.

And here in this uncostly nest,
These little creatures have been blest;
Nor have kings known in palaces
Half their contentedness in this —
Poor simple dwelling as it is!
— *Mary Howitt.*

THE WILD RABBITS.

AMONG the sand-hills,
   Near by the sea,
Wild young rabbits
   Were seen by me.

They live in burrows
   With winding ways,
And there they shelter
   On rainy days.

The mother rabbits
  Make cosy nests,
With hairy linings
  From their breasts.

The tender young ones
  Are nursed and fed,
And safely hidden
  In this warm bed.

And when they are older,
  They all come out
Upon the sand-hills,
  And frisk about.

They play, and nibble
  The long, dry grass,
But scamper away
  Whenever you pass.

—*Selected.*

CORN.

THERE is a plant you often see
  In gardens and in fields;
Its stalk is straight, its leaves are long,
  And precious fruit it yields.

The fruit, when young, is soft and white,
  And closely wrapped in green,
And tassels hang from every ear,
  Which children love to glean.

But when the tassels fade away
    The fruit is ripe and old;
It peeps from out the wrapping dry,
    Like beads of yellow gold.

The fruit, when young, we boil and roast,
    When old, we grind it well.
Now, think of all the plants you know,
    And try its name to tell.

—Selected.

A LESSON.

A CORN-STALK glanced down at some grasses,
    And said in an arrogant tone,
"I wish that my fawning relations
    Would move off and leave me alone.

"Just see how they mix with the clovers,
    And nod at their red and white crests;
And even the poor silly daisies
    They're ready to welcome as guests!

"No wonder each morn when they waken,
    Their eyelids are heavy with tears,
Through envy of my rustling raiment,
    And the gold drops that shine in my ears.

"'Tis true, we've a common venation;
    But that need not addle their brains;
They're born to a lowly position,
    There's no blood of mine in their veins."

With that she threw back her silk tassels,
   And left them to wave in the breeze,
Nor took farther note of the grasses
   That timidly crouched at her knees.

In autumn a reaper discovered
   The corn-husk all withered and dried,
So he stripped off her bright golden ear-drops
   And ruthlessly cast her aside;

And when the next spring's glowing sunshine
   Caused Nature her white robe to doff,
And the earth showed a few snowy patches,
   Like a cake with the frosting picked off;

I said of the pale, slender fingers
   That the roots of the grasses sent forth,
"Ah, surely, the proud are made stubble,
   And the meek shall inherit the earth!"

—Selected.

THE CHILD AND THE WORLD.

I SEE a nest in a green elm-tree
   With little brown sparrows,—one, two, three!
The elm-tree stretches its branches wide,
And the nest is soft and warm inside.
At morn the sun, so golden bright,
Climbs up to fill the world with light;
It opens the flowers, it wakens me,
And wakens the birdies,—one, two, three.
And leaning out of my window high,
I look far up at the blue, blue sky,

And then far out at the earth so green,
And think it the loveliest ever seen, —
The loveliest world that ever was seen!

But by and by, when the sun is low,
And birds and babies sleepy grow,
I peep again from my window high,
And look at the earth and clouds and sky
The night dew falls in silent showers,
To cool the hearts of thirsty flowers;
The moon comes out, — the slender thing,
A crescent yet, but soon a ring, —
And brings with her one yellow star;
How small it looks, away so far!
But soon, in the heaven's shining blue,
A thousand twinkle and blink at you,
Like a thousand lamps in the sky so blue.

And hush! a light breeze stirs the tree,
And rocks the birdies, — one, two, three.
What a beautiful cradle, that soft, warm nest!
What a dear little coverlid, mamma-bird's breast!
She's hugging them close to her, tight, so tight
That each downy head is hid from sight;
But out from under her sheltering wings
Their bright eyes glisten, the cunning things!
I lean far out from my window's height
And say, " Dear, lovely world, good-night!

" Good-night, dear, pretty, baby moon!
Your cradle you'll outgrow quite soon,
And then, perhaps, all night you'll shine,
A grown-up lady moon! so fine

And bright that all the stars
Will want to light their lamps from yours.
Sleep sweetly, birdies, never fear,
For God is always watching near!
And you, dear, friendly world above,
The same One holds us in His love;
Both you so great, and I so small,
Are safe, — He sees the sparrows fall,
The dear God watcheth over all!"

— *Selected.*

A NATIONAL FLOWER.

THEY ask me to vote for a national flower;
   Now, which will it be, I wonder.
To settle the question is out of my power,
   But I'd rather not make a blunder.

And I love the Mayflower the best in May,
   Smiling up from its snow-drift cover,
With its breath that is sweet as a kiss to say
   That the reign of winter is over.

And I love the goldenrod, too, for its gold,
   And because through autumn it lingers,
And offers more wealth than his hands can hold
   To the grasp of the poor man's fingers.

I should vote for them both if I might;
   But I do not feel positive whether
The flowers themselves would be neighborly quite, —
   Pink and yellow don't go together.

Oh, yes, but they do! In the breezy wild rose,
   The darlingest daughter of summer,
Whose heart with the sun's yellow gold overflows,
   And whose blushes so well become her.

Instead of one flower I will vote for three;
   The Mayflowers know that I mean them,
And the goldenrod surely my choice will be,
   With the sweet brier-rose between them.

You see I'm impartial, I've no way but this.
   My vote, with a rhyme and a reason,
For the Mayflower, the wild rose, and goldenrod is,
   A blossom for every season.
                                 — *Lucy Larcom.*

TWO WISE OWLS.

WE are two dusky owls, and we live in a tree;
       Look at her, — look at me!
Look at her, — she's my mate, and the mother of three
       Pretty owlets, and we
Have a warm cosy nest, just as snug as can be.

We are both very wise; for our heads, as you see,
       (Look at her, — look at me!)
Are as large as the heads of four birds ought to be,
       And our horns, you'll agree,
Make us look wiser still, sitting here on the tree.

Far away in the valley, a mile it may be,
       Is a churchyard, and we

Often sit there at midnight, and hoot in high glee.
>Does that owl look like me?
For the bird in the air is my mate, as you see.

And we care not how gloomy the night-time may be;
>We can see, — we can see
Through the forest to roam, — it suits her, it suits me;
>And we're free, — we are free
To bring back what we find, to our nest in the tree.
>*— Selected.*

TOM.

YES, Tom's the best fellow that ever you knew,
>Just listen to this: —
When the old mill took fire, and the flooring fell through,
And I with it, helpless, — there, full in my view,
What do you think my eyes saw through the fire
That crept along, crept along, nigher and nigher,
But Robin, my baby boy, laughing to see
The shining? He must have come there after me.
Toddled alone from the cottage without
Any one's missing him. Then what a shout—
Oh! how I shouted, "For Heaven's sake, men,
Save little Robin!" Again and again
They tried, but the fire held them back like a wall,
I could hear them go at it, and at it, and call,
"Never mind, baby, sit still like a man!
We're coming to get you as fast as we can."
They could not see him, but I could; he sat
Still on a beam, his little straw hat

Carefully placed by his side; and his eyes
Stared at the flame with a baby's surprise,
Calm and unconscious, as nearer it crept;
The roar of the fire up above must have kept
From reaching the child. But I heard it.
      It came,
Again and again. O God, what a cry!
The axes went faster; I saw the sparks fly
Where the men worked like tigers, nor minded the heat
That scorched them, — when suddenly, there at their feet,
The great beam leaned in — they saw him — then, crash,
Down came the wall! The men made a dash, —
Jumped to get out of the way, — and I thought
"All's up with poor little Robin!" and brought
Slowly the arm that was least hurt to hide
The sight of the child there, — when swift at my side
Some one rushed by, and went right through the flame,
Straight as a dart, — caught the child and then came
Back with him, choking and crying, but — saved!
Saved safe and sound!
      Oh, how the men raved,
Shouted and cried, and hurrahed! Then they all
Rushed at the work again, lest the back wall,
Where I was lying away from the fire,
Should fall in and bury me.
      Oh! you'd admire
To see Robin now; he's as bright as a dime,
Deep in some mischief, too, most of the time;
Tom, it was, saved him. Now, isn't it true
Tom's the best fellow that ever you knew?
There's Robin now! See, he's strong as a log!
And there comes Tom, too —
      Yes, Tom was our dog.
     — *Constance Fenimore Woolson.*

THE RAINY DAY.

THE day is cold, and dark, and dreary;
It rains, and the wind is never weary;
The vine still clings to the moldering wall,
But at every gust the dead leaves fall,
  And the day is dark and dreary.

My life is cold, and dark, and dreary;
It rains, and the wind is never weary;
My thoughts still cling to the moldering past,
But the hopes of youth fall thick in the blast,
  And the days must be dark and dreary.

Be still, sad heart! and cease repining;
Behind the clouds is the sun still shining;
Thy fate is the common fate of all,
Into each life some rain must fall,
  Some days must be dark and dreary.
                —*Henry Wadsworth Longfellow.*

NOVEMBER.

THE leaves are fading and falling,
  The winds are rough and wild,
The birds have ceased their calling,
  But let me tell you, my child,

Though day by day, as it closes,
  Doth darker and colder grow,
The roots of the bright red roses
  Will keep alive in the snow.

And when the winter is over,
  The boughs will get new leaves;
The quail come back to the clover,
  And the swallow back to the eaves.

The robin will wear on his bosom
  A vest that is bright and new,
And the loveliest wayside blossom
  Will shine with the sun and dew.

The leaves, to-day, are whirling,
  The brooks are all dry and dumb;
But let me tell you, my darling,
  The spring will be sure to come.

There must be rough, cold weather,
  And winds and rains so wild;
Not all good things together
  Come to us here, my child.

So, when some dear joy loses
  Its beauteous summer glow,
Think how the roots of the roses
  Are kept alive in the snow.
—*Alice Cary.*

THANKSGIVING DAY.

OVER the river and through the wood,
  To grandfather's house we'll go;
    The horse knows the way
    To carry the sleigh
  Through the white and drifted snow.

Over the river and through the wood, —
  Oh, how the wind does blow!
    It stings the toes,
    And bites the nose
  As over the ground we go.

Over the river and through the wood,
  To have a first-rate play,
    Hear the bells ring
    "Ting-a-ling-ding!"
  Hurrah for Thanksgiving Day!

Over the river and through the wood
  Trot fast, my dapple gray!
    Spring over the ground
    Like a hunting hound!
  For this is Thanksgiving Day.

Over the river and through the wood,
  And straight through the barn-yard gate;
    We seem to go
    Extremely slow;
  It is so hard to wait!

Over the river and through the wood,
  Now grandmother's cap I spy!
    Hurrah for the fun!
    Is the pudding done?
  Hurrah for the pumpkin pie!
                — *Lydia Maria Child.*

THE RACCOON.

COME, child, and see our pet raccoon, —
    The raccoons live in the woods, you know,
  But ours was caught
  And caged, and brought
From old Virginia, long ago.

Oh, no, you need not be afraid;
See, he is fastened with a chain;
  For ropes enough
  He has gnawed off,
And he is hard to catch again.

He e'en will climb this ten-foot fence,
And, careless where his feet may strike,
  He tumbles, bang!
  And there will hang,
His rope being caught by vine or spike.

So now he's chained; yet up he'll climb
The stake to which he's fastened tight,
  And mutter low,
  So pleading, Oh!
'Twould make you sorry for him, quite.

Just see his nose, so pointed, sharp, —
His ears as keen as keen can be, —
  His eyes so bright,
  So full of light,
And see him leap right merrily!

His fur, you see, is yellowish gray, —
And he is nearly two feet long;
   He lives on roots,
   And nuts and fruits,
When he's his native woods among.

But here we give him bread and milk;
He never eats like dogs or lambs,
   But takes it up
   From out the cup
With his fore feet, as we use hands.

You'd laugh to see him, I am sure;
Of strawberries, too, he's very fond;
   Will poke around
   Till he has found
Each one among the hulls out-thrown.
                — *Mother Truth's Melodies.*

THE ANT AN ENGINEER.

THE pastry was delicious, and I wanted it myself,
   So I put it in the pantry on the very lowest shelf;
And to keep it from the insects, those ants so red and small,
I made a river round it of molasses, best of all.

But the enemy approached it, all as hungry as could be,
And the captain, with his aide-de-camp, just skirmished round to see

Whether they could ford the river or should try some
    other plan,
And, together with his comrades, he around the liquid ran.

To his joy and satisfaction, after traveling around,
The place where the molasses was the narrowest he found;
Then again he reconnoitered, rushing forward and then
    back,
Till he spied some loosened plaster in the wall around a
    tack.

He divided then his forces, with a foreman for each squad,
And he marshaled the whole army and before him each
    ant trod;
His directions all were given; to his chiefs he gave a call,
While he headed the procession as they marched off up
    the wall.

Every ant then seized his plaster, just a speck and nothing
    more,
And he climbed and tugged and carried till he'd brought
    it to the shore;
Then they built their bridge, just working for an hour by
    the sky,
After which they all marched over and all fell to eating
    pie.

—*Selected.*

THE DAY IS DONE.

THE day is done, and the darkness
    Falls from the wings of Night,
As a feather is wafted downward
    From an eagle in his flight.

I see the lights of the village
   Gleam through the rain and the mist,
And a feeling of sadness comes o'er me
   That my soul cannot resist:

A feeling of sadness and longing,
   That is not akin to pain,
And resembles sorrow only
   As the mist resembles the rain.

Come, read to me some poem,
   Some simple and heartfelt lay,
That shall soothe this restless feeling,
   And banish the thoughts of day.

Not from the grand old masters,
   Not from the bards sublime,
Whose distant footsteps echo
   Through the corridors of Time.

For, like strains of martial music,
   Their mighty thoughts suggest
Life's endless toil and endeavor;
   And to-night I long for rest.

Read from some humbler poet,
   Whose songs gushed from his heart,
As showers from the clouds of summer,
   Or tears from the eyelids start;

Who, through long days of labor,
   And nights devoid of ease,
Still heard from his soul the music
   Of wonderful melodies.

Such songs have power to quiet
    The restless pulse of care,
And come like the benediction
    That follows after prayer.

Then read from the treasured volume
    The poem of thy choice,
And lend to the rhyme of the poet
    The beauty of thy voice.

And the night shall be filled with music,
    And the cares, that infest the day,
Shall fold their tents like the Arabs,
    And as silently steal away.
                — *Henry Wadsworth Longfellow.*

THE SETTING SUN.

DEAR John, the sun is setting now;
    Behold him in the west;
And all the children now must soon
    Lie down and go to rest.

In other countries far away,
    The day begins to break,
And many a child and many a bird
    Will soon be wide awake.

But when the sun comes round again,
    And rises in our east,
Then evening will begin with them,
    And they to bed will haste.

How very good in God it is,
    To make the sun to go
All round this great, wide world of ours,
    To light each country so.
—Selected.

AT SUNSET.

SUNSET glories are smiling down;
    Blue and crimson and golden brown.
Full many a twittering note is heard;
The good-night carol of many a bird.

The flowers are glad at sunset time,
The yellow aster and fragrant thyme;
The purple pansy lifts its head,
Its petals half-dropping and withered and dead.

Baby laughs at the colors red
And gray and purple, and shakes her head.
"Just right for a dress, mamma, don't you see?
It's plenty enough for you and me."

Grandpa sits in the twilight gray,
His locks are white as the moonbeam's ray,
His brow is furrowed with age and care,
His smile is sweet as angels wear.

Grandpa and baby watch together
The flowers and sunset and starry weather.
The one, for a glorious harvest meet;
The other, like sunbeam at his feet.

We are all children, scarce can tell
Of the wonderful things we love so well;
Even the aged, with locks like snow,
God gave them to us, is all we know.

After the sunset the stars shine down
Where once was crimson and blue and brown;
The full-orbed moon in silvery white, —
And dusky shadows are clothed in light.

Beyond earth's sunset glories fair
Lies a golden daylight, deep and rare.
And, listen! — through its hush, are heard,
Sweetest of carols from twittering bird.
—*Mattie A. W. Clark.*

TWINKLE, TWINKLE.

"TWINKLE, twinkle, little star,
Up above the world so far,
Whisper now and tell me, pray,
What you are, and how you stay."

"Some of us away so far,
Planets like your own earth are,
And we shine with borrowed light,
Borrowed from the sun so bright;

"Some of us are silvery moons,
Shining all the nightly noons;
Some of us are jelly soft,
Shooting, falling, from aloft;

"Some of us are nebulæ, —
Faint and misty stars we be;
Some are suns to other worlds;
Here and there a comet whirls;

"Having each our time and place,
Swinging in the wondrous space;
Held in line by Him who planned,
And who holds you in His hand."
—*Mother Truth's Melodies.*

THE NEW MOON.

DEAR mother, how pretty
   The moon looks to-night!
She was never so cunning before;
   Her two little horns
   Are so sharp and bright,
I hope she'll not grow any more.

   If I were up there,
   With you and my friends,
I'd rock in it nicely, you'd see;
   I'd sit in the middle
   And hold by both ends;
Oh, what a bright cradle 'twould be!

   I would call to the stars
   To keep out of the way,
Lest we should rock over their toes;
   And then I would rock
   Till the dawn of the day,
And see where the pretty moon goes.

And there we would stay
In the beautiful skies;
And through the bright clouds we would roam.
We would see the sun set,
And see the sun rise,
And on the next rainbow come home.

—*Mrs. Follen.*

A NAUGHTY LITTLE COMET.

THERE was a little comet who lived near the Milky Way;
She loved to wander out at night, and jump about and play.

The mother of the comet was a very good old star;
She used to scold her reckless child for venturing out too far.

She told her of the ogre Sun, who loved on stars to sup,
And who asked no better pastime than gobbling comets up.

But instead of growing cautious, and of showing proper fear,
The foolish little comet edged up nearer and more near.

She switched her saucy trail along right where the sun could see,
And flirted with old Mars, and was as bold as bold could be.

She laughed to scorn the quiet stars who never frisked about;
She said there was no fun in life unless you ventured out.

She liked to make the planets stare, and wished no better mirth
Than just to see the telescopes aimed at her from the Earth.

She wondered how so many stars could mope through nights and days,
And let the sickly-faced old Moon get all the love and praise.

And as she talked and tossed her head and switched her shining trail,
The staid old mother-star grew sad, her cheek grew wan and pale;

For she had lived there in the skies a million years or more,
And she had heard gay comets talk in just this way before.

And by and by there came an end to this gay comet's fun;
She went a tiny bit too far, and vanished in the Sun!

But quiet stars she laughed to scorn are twinkling every night.
No more she swings her shining trail before the whole world's sight.

— *Ella Wheeler Wilcox.*

NORSE LULLABY.

THE sky is dark and the hills are white,
  As the storm-king speeds from the north to-night;
And this is the song the storm-king sings,
As over the world his cloak he flings:

"Sleep, sleep, little one, sleep;"
He rustles his wings, and gruffly sings:
"Sleep, little one, sleep."

On yonder mountain-side a vine
Clings at the foot of a mother pine;
The tree bends over the trembling thing.
And only the vine can hear her sing:
"Sleep, sleep, little one, sleep;
What shall you fear when I am here?
Sleep, little one, sleep."

The king may sing in his bitter flight,
The tree may croon to the vine to-night,
But the little snowflake at my breast
Liketh the song I sing the best,—
· Sleep, sleep, little one, sleep;
Weary thou art, anext my heart;
Sleep, little one, sleep.
— *Eugene Field* — *A Little Book of Western Verse.*

"HO, FOR SLUMBERLAND!"

A LITTLE song for bedtime, when, robed in gowns of white,
All sleepy little children set sail across the night
For that pleasant, pleasant country, where the pretty dream-flowers blow,
'Twixt the sunset and the sunrise,—
" For the Slumber Islands, ho!"

When the little ones get drowsy, and heavy lids droop down
To hide blue eyes and black eyes, gray eyes, and eyes of brown,
A thousand boats for Dreamland are waiting in a row,
And the ferrymen are calling,
    "For the Slumber Islands, ho!"

Then the sleepy little children fill the boats along the shore,
And go sailing off to Dreamland; and the dipping of the oar
In the sea of Sleep makes music that the children only know
When they answer to the boatmen's
    "For the Slumber Islands, ho!"

Oh! take a kiss, my darlings, ere you sail away from me
In the boat of dreams that's waiting to bear you o'er the sea;
Take a kiss, and give one, and then away you go,
A-sailing into Dreamland,—
    "For the Slumber Islands, ho!"
    — *Eben E. Rexford — St. Nicholas.*

CAN YOU COUNT THE STARS?

CAN you count the stars that brightly
 Twinkle in the midnight sky?
Can you count the clouds, so lightly
 O'er the meadows floating by?

God the Lord doth mark their number
With his eyes that never slumber.
He hath made them, ev'ry one.

Do you know how many children
   Rise each morning, blithe and gay?
Can you count the little voices,
   Singing sweetly, day by day?
God hears all the little voices,
In their pretty songs rejoices,
He doth love them, ev'ry one.

—Selected.

SONGS OF WINTER.

"We haven't a nest,
 Nor a place of rest,
 Save this oak-tree bending down."

Songs of Winter.

MORNING HYMN.

 FATHER, Thou art near — so near
   Thy children while they work or play;
Thine arms enfold us tenderly,
   O help us please Thee day by day!

The little flowers — we love them so —
   Along the hillside and the dell,
With faces fair upturned to Thee,
   Sweetly to us Thy goodness tell.

The little birds that love to trill
   Their music over morn and night,
The breaking waves along the shore,
   Teach us to praise Thee with delight.

The snowflakes dropping down from heaven
   So swiftly and so silently,
The lilies gleaming on the lake,
   Teach us Thy spotless purity.

Father, all things together sing —
   The earth below, the skies above,
And all the airs that round us breathe —
   The fullness of Thy watchful love.

—Selected.

BIRD WITH BOSOM RED.

WHEN the winds of winter blow,
And the air is thick with snow,
Drifting over hill and hollow,
Whitening all the naked trees —
Then the bluebird and the jay
And the oriole fly away,
Where the bobolink and swallow
Flew before them, at their ease.

But we are not left alone,
Though the summer birds have flown;
Though the honey-bees have vanished,
And the katydids are dead;
Still a cheery, ringing note,
From a dear, melodious throat,
Tells that winter has not banished
Little bird with bosom red.

Pipe away, you happy bird,
Sweeter song I never heard;
For it seems to say: " Remember
God, our Father, sits above —
Though the world is full of wrong,
Though the winter days are long —
He can fill the bleak December
With the sunshine of His love."

—*Selected*

THE FOUR WINDS.

IN winter, when the wind I hear,
   I know the clouds will disappear;
For 'tis the wind who sweeps the sky
And piles the snow in ridges high.

In spring, when stirs the wind, I know
That soon the crocus buds will show;
For 'tis the wind who bids them wake
And into pretty blossoms break.

In summer, when it softly blows,
Soon red, I know, will be the rose;
For 'tis the wind to her who speaks,
And brings the blushes to her cheeks.

In autumn, when the wind is up,
I know the acorn's out its cup;
For 'tis the wind who takes it out,
And plants an oak somewhere about.
— Frank Dempster Sherman.

WHAT THE WINDS BRING.

"WHICH is the wind that brings the cold?"
   "The north wind, Freddy, and all the snow,
And the sheep will scamper into the fold
   When the north begins to blow."

"Which is the wind that brings the heat?"
"The south wind, Katy; and corn will grow,
And peaches redden for you to eat,
When the south begins to blow."

"Which is the wind that brings the rain?"
"The east wind, Arty; and farmers know
That cows come shivering up the lane,
When the east begins to blow."

"Which is the wind that brings the flowers?"
"The west wind, Bessy; and soft and low
The birdies sing in the summer hours,
When the west begins to blow."
— *E. C. Stedman.*

THE FOG.

"WHAT is the fog, mamma?"
"Sometimes the air is light,
And cannot bear up all the mists,
And then 'tis foggy, quite;
But when air heavier grows,
The fog is borne above,
And floated off, the cloudy stuff,
Just see it, graceful, move."
— *Mother Truth's Melodies.*

THE RAIN.

"WHAT makes the rain, mamma?"
   "The mists and vapor rise
From land and stream and rolling sea,
   Up toward the distant skies;
And there they form the clouds,
   Which, when they're watery, dear,
Pour all the water down to earth,
   And rain afar or near."
              —Mother Truth's Melodies.

THE LITTLE ARTIST.

OH, there is a little artist
   Who paints in the cold night hours
Pictures for wee, wee children,
   Of wondrous trees and flowers,—

Pictures of snow-capped mountains
   Touching the snow-white sky;
Pictures of distant oceans,
   Where pygmy ships sail by;

Pictures of rushing rivers,
   By fairy bridges spanned;
Bits of beautiful landscapes,
   Copied from elfin land.

The moon is the lamp he paints by,
   His canvas the window-pane,
His brush is a frozen snowflake;
   Jack Frost is the artist's name.
                                 —*Selected.*

JACK FROST.

"Some one has been in the garden,
   Nipping the flowers so fair;
All the green leaves are withered;
   Now, who do you think has been there?

"Some one has been in the forest,
   Cracking the chestnut burrs;
Who is it dropping the chestnuts,
   Whenever a light wind stirs?

"Some one has been on the hilltop,
   Chipping the moss-covered rocks;
Who has been cracking and breaking
   Them into fragments and blocks?

"Some one has been at the windows,
   Marking on every pane;
Who made those glittering pictures
   Of lace-work, fir-trees, and grain?

"Some one is all the time working
   Out on the pond so blue,
Bridging it over with crystal;
   Who is it, now? Can you tell who?

"While his good bridge he is building,
  We will keep guard at the gate;
And when he has it all finished,
  Hurrah for the boys that can skate!

"Let him work on: we are ready;
  Not much for our fun does it cost!
Three cheers for the bridge he is making!
  And three, with a will, for Jack Frost!"
— *Selected.*

FROST PICTURES.

PICTURES on the window,
  Painted by Jack Frost,
Coming at the midnight,
  With the noon are lost;
Here a row of fir-trees,
  Standing straight and tall;
There a rapid river,
  And a waterfall.

Here a branch of coral
  From the briny sea;
There a weary traveler
  Resting 'neath a tree;
Here a grand old iceberg,
  Floating slowly on;
There a mighty forest
  Of the torrid zone.

Here a swamp, all tangled, —
   Rushes, ferns, and brake;
There a rugged mountain,
   Here a little lake.
Then a breath, the lightest
   Floating in the air,
Jack Frost catches quickly,
   And imprints it there.

And thus you are painting,
   Little children, too,
On your life's fair window
   Always something new;
But your little pictures
   Will not pass away
Like those Jack Frost's fingers
   Paint each winter day.

Each kind word or action
   Is a picture bright;
Every duty mastered
   Is lovely in the light;
But each thought of anger,
   Every word of strife,
Blemishes the picture,
   Stains the glass of life.

Then be very careful,
   Every day and hour,
Lest unseemly touches
   Trace your window o'er;
Let the lines be always
   Made by kindness bright, —
Paint your glass with pictures
   Of the true and right.

—Selected.

THE FROST.

THE Frost looked forth one still, clear night,
   And whispered, "Now I shall be out of sight;
So through the valley and over the height,
   In silence I'll take my way;
I will not go on like that blustering train,
The wind and the snow, the hail and the rain,
Who makes so much bustle and noise in vain,
   But I'll be as busy as they!"

Then he flew to the mountain, and powdered its crest;
He lit on the trees, and their boughs he drest
In diamond beads; and over the breast
   Of the quivering lake he spread
A coat of mail, that it need not fear
The downward point of many a spear,
That he hung on its margin, far and near,
   Where a rock could rear its head.

He went to the windows of those who slept,
And over each pane like a fairy crept;
Wherever he breathed, wherever he stepped,
   By the light of the morn were seen
Most beautiful things; there were flowers and trees;
There were bevies of birds and swarms of bees;
There were cities with temples and towers; and these
   All pictured in silver sheen!

But he did one thing that was hardly fair,—
He peeped in the cupboard, and finding there
That all had forgotten for him to prepare,
   "Now, just to set them a-thinking,

I'll bite this basket of fruit," said he,
"This costly pitcher I'll burst in three;
And the glass of water they've left for me
   Shall 'tchick!' to tell them I'm drinking!"
—Hannah F. Gould.

LITTLE SNOWFLAKES.

THE snowflakes fall so gently,
   You ne'er can hear a sound,
As sailing through the frosty air
   They nestle on the ground.
They form a carpet, soft and white,
   For merry little feet,
While cheeks grow round and rosy,
   And laughter is so sweet.

Some children are like snowflakes,—
   Their step is light and low,
And when they walk from place to place,
   You ne'er can hear them go.
Oh, let us be like snowflakes,
   So soft and pure and bright,
And when God looks into our souls,
   He'll see a pleasing sight.
—M. M.

HELP ONE ANOTHER.

"HELP one another," the snowflakes said,
    As they cuddled down in their fleecy bed.
"One of us here would not be felt,
One of us here would quickly melt;
But I'll help you, and you help me,
And then what a splendid drift there'll be."

"Help one another," the maple spray
Said to its fellow-leaves one day;
"The sun would wither me here alone,
Long enough ere the day is gone;
But I'll help you, and you help me,
And then what a splendid shade there'll be."

"Help one another," the dewdrop cried,
Seeing another drop close to its side;
"The warm south wind would dry me away,
And I should be gone ere noon to-day;
But I'll help you, and you help me,
And we'll make a brook and run to the sea."

"Help one another," a grain of sand
Said to another grain close at hand;
"The wind may carry me over the sea,
And then, oh, what will become of me?
But come, my brother, give me your hand,
We'll build a mountain and then we'll stand."

And so the snowflakes grew to drifts;
The grains of sand to a mountain;
The leaves became a summer shade;
The dewdrops fed a fountain.

—Selected.

LITTLE SNOWFLAKES.

STILL and gentle all around,
    Little snowflakes, soft and light
One by one spread o'er the ground,
    Making it a fleecy white.

As we watch these little flakes,
    Falling down so small and light,
Who would think so few it takes
    Thus to form this robe of white?

Just like them are duties done,
    Still and gentle, every hour;
Smallest deeds, we early learn,
    Give to life its greatest power.
—*Selected.*

THE FIRST SNOW.

THE north wind doth blow, and we shall have snow,
    And what will poor robin do then, poor thing?
He'll sit in the barn and keep himself warm,
    And hide his head under his wing, poor thing.

The north wind doth blow, and we shall have snow,
    And what will the honey bee do, poor thing?
In his hive he will stay till the cold's passed away,
    And then he'll come out in the spring, poor thing.

The north wind doth blow, and we shall have snow,
    And what will the dormouse do then, poor thing?
Rolled up like a ball in his nest, snug and small,
    He'll sleep till warm weather comes back, poor thing.

The north wind doth blow, and we shall have snow,
    And what will the children do then, poor things?
When lessons are done they'll jump, skip, and run,
    And that's how they'll keep themselves warm, poor things.

—Selected.

THE SNOW-SHOWER.

"SEE, mamma, the crumbs are flying
    Fast and thickly through the air;
On the branches they are lying,
    On the walks and everywhere.
Oh, how glad the birds will be,
When so many crumbs they see."

"No, my little girl, 'tis snowing,
    Nothing for the birds is here;
Very cold the air is growing,
    'Tis the winter of the year;
Frost will nip the robins' food,
'Twill no more be sweet and good.

"See the clouds the skies that cover,
    'Tis from them the snowflakes fall,
Whitening hills and fields all over,
    Hanging from the fir-trees tall.
Were it warm, 'twould rain; but lo!
Frost has changed the rain to snow."

"If the robins food are needing,
  Oh, I hope to me they'll come;
I should like to see them feeding,
  On the window of my room;
I'll divide with them my store;
Much I wish I could do more."

— *Mary Lundie Duncan.*

LITTLE SHIPS IN THE AIR.

"Flakes of snow, with sails so white,
  Drifting down the wintry skies,
Tell me where your route begins,
  Say which way your harbor lies?"

"In the clouds, the roomy clouds,
  Arching earth with shadowy dome,
There's the port from which we sail,
  There is tiny snowflake's home."

"And the cargo that you take
  From those cloudy ports above —
Is it always meant to bless,
  Sent in anger or in love?"

"Warmth for all the tender roots,
  Warmth for every living thing,
Water for the rivers' flow,
  This the cargo that we bring."

"Who's the Master that you serve,
  Bids you lift your tiny sails,

Brings you safely to the earth,
  Guides you through the wintry gales?"

"He who tells the birds to sing,
  He who sends the April flowers,
He who ripens all the fruit,
  That great Master, he is ours."
      —*E. A. Rand.*

THE SNOW-SHOWER.

STAND here by my side and turn, I pray,
  On the lake below thy gentle eyes;
The clouds hang over it heavy and gray,
  And dark and silent the water lies;
And out of that frozen mist the snow,
In wavering flakes, begins to flow;
    Flake after flake,
They sink in the dark and silent lake.

See how in a living swarm they come
  From the chambers beyond that misty veil;
Some hover awhile in air, and some
  Rush prone from the sky like summer hail.
All, dropping swiftly, or settling slow,
Meet, and are still in the depths below;
    Flake after flake,
Dissolved in the dark and silent lake.

Here delicate snow-stars, out of the cloud,
  Come floating downward in airy play,

Like spangles dropped from the glistening crowd,
   That whiten by night the milky way;
There broader and burlier masses fall;
The sullen water buries them all —
     Flake after flake —
All drowned in the dark and silent lake.

And some, as on tender wings they glide
   From their chilly birth-cloud, dim and gray,
Are joined in their fall, and, side by side,
   Come clinging along their unsteady way;
As friend with friend, or husband with wife,
Makes hand in hand the passage of life;
     Each mated flake
Soon sinks in the dark and silent lake.

Lo! while we are gazing, in swifter haste
   Stream down the snows, till the air is white,
As, myriads by myriads madly chased,
   They fling themselves from their shadowy height.
The fair frail creatures of middle sky,
What speed they make, with their grave so nigh;
     Flake after flake,
To lie in the dark and silent lake!

I see in thy gentle eyes a tear;
   They turn to me in sorrowful thought;
Thou thinkest of friends, the good and dear,
   Who were for a time, and now are not;
Like those fair children of cloud and frost,
That glisten a moment and then are lost,
     Flake after flake —
All lost in the dark and silent lake.

Yet look again, for the clouds divide;
  A gleam of blue on the water lies;
And far away, on the mountain side,
  A sunbeam falls from the opening skies.
But the hurrying host that flew between
The cloud and the water, no more is seen;
    Flake after flake,
At rest in the dark and silent lake.
—*William Cullen Bryant.*

THE SNOW-STORM.

WE are free! we are free! the snowflakes cried,
  Hurrah! hurrah! away we hide.
Now we're whirling, and twirling, and dancing around,
And gently sinking to the ground.
The jolly north wind! how he makes us fly,
And whistles the tune we are dancing by.
We cover the valleys, we cover the hills,
We bury the flowers and frozen rills,
We're dashing out this way, and that way again,
We're dashing against the window pane.
Then away, away, away, away,
We'll make a track for the merry sleigh;
We're drifting high, ah! ah! here's fun
For the boys and girls
When school is done.
Now we're whirling, and twirling, and dancing around,
And gently sinking to the ground.
—*Selected.*

THE DISAPPOINTED SNOWFLAKES.

FOUR and twenty snowflakes came tumbling from the
   sky,
And said, " Let's make a snow drift—
  We can if we but try."
So down they gently fluttered
  And lighted on the ground,
And when they were all seated
  They sadly looked around.
"We're very few indeed," sighed they,
  " And we sometimes make mistakes;
We cannot make a snowdrift
  With four and twenty flakes."
Just then the sun peeped round a cloud
  And smiled at the array,
And the disappointed snowflakes
  Melted quietly away.

—Selected.

IT SNOWS! IT SNOWS!

IT snows! yes, it snows! and the children are wild,
  At thought of the fun in the snow-drifts up-piled;
The boy with his first new boots is in sight,
And the wee baby-girl, with her mittens so bright.
They are tramping and tossing the snow as they run,
And laughing and shouting, so brimful of fun;
While the ten-year-old twins, in a somersault mood,
Have measured their length from the barn to the wood,
A dozen times, yes, or it may be a score,
Till their cheeks are as red as the roses, and more;

Then the elfin of twelve and the boy of fifteen
Are pelting each other with snowballs so keen,
That we, who are older, forget to be staid,
And shout, each with each, as the youngsters, arrayed
In feathery garments, press on or retreat,
Determined to win, nor acknowledge defeat.
But the children, at length, tired out with their play,
And stamping the snow from their feet by the way,
Come slipping and stumbling and scrambling along,
While the big brother catching the baby-girl's song,
"Oh, my finders are told!" gives her now a gay toss,
The golden hair streaming like distaff of floss; —
And so cheery the group that is ranged round the board,
That for snow, blessed snow, we all thank the good Lord.
— *Mother Truth's Melodies.*

SNOW.

SNOW so fair,
   Snow so fair,
Whirling through the wintry air!
Dropping down,
Dropping down,
On the busy town,
Do you, white-robed fairies, say,
Dance in honor of the day?
Snow so fair,
Snow so fair,
Dancing through the air!

Wind so cold,
Wind so cold,
Did you know this hero bold?

NATURE IN VERSE.

Breezes strong,
Breezes strong,
Sweeping swift along,
Do your trumpets blow for him,
In the forests dark and dim?
Breezes strong,
Breezes strong,
Sweeping swift along.

Pretty star,
Pretty star,
Beaming at us from afar,
Smiling down,
Smiling down,
On the busy town,
Have you lit your lamp so bright
Just in honor of the night?
Pretty star,
Pretty star,
Beaming from afar.

— *A. E. C.* — *Popular Educator.*

THE SNOW-BIRD.

IN the morning light trills the gay swallow,
    The thrush in the roses below,
The meadow-lark sings in the meadow,
    And the snow-bird sings in the snow.
        "Twee wee!
        Chickadee!"
The snow-bird sings in the snow.

The blue martin trills in the gable,
　　The wren on the ground below,
In the elm flutes the golden robin,
　　But the snow-bird sings in the snow.
　　　　"Twee wee!
　　　　Chickadee!"
　　The snow-bird sings in the snow.

High wheels the gray wing of the osprey,
　　The wing of the sparrow drops low,
In the mist dips the wing of the robin,
　　And the snow-bird's wing in the snow.
　　　　"Twee wee!
　　　　Chickadee!"
　　The snow-bird sings in the snow.

I love the high heart of the osprey,
　　The meek heart of the thrush below,
The heart of the lark in the meadow,
　　And the snow-bird's heart in the snow;
　　　　But dearest to me
　　　　"Chickadee! Chickadee!"
　　Is that true little heart in the snow.
　　　　　　　　　　　　— *Selected.*

THE SNOW-BIRD'S SONG.

THE ground was all covered with snow one day,
　　And two little sisters were busy at play,
When a snow-bird came flitting close by on a tree,
And merrily singing his chick-a-dee-dee,
　　Chick-a-dee-dee, chick-a-dee-dee,
And merrily singing his chick-a-dee-dee.

He had not been singing that tune very long,
Ere Emily heard him, so loud was his song;
"Oh, sister, look out of the window," said she,
"Here's a dear little bird singing chick-a-dee-dee.
    Chick-a-dee-dee, chick-a-dee-dee,
And merrily singing his chick-a-dee-dee.

"Oh, mother, do get him some stockings and shoes,
And a nice little frock, and a hat if you choose;
I wish he'd come into the parlor, and see
How warm we would make him, poor chick-a-dee-dee."
    Chick-a-dee-dee, chick-a-dee-dee,
And merrily singing his chick-a-dee-dee.

"There is One, my dear child, though I cannot tell who,
Has clothed me already, and warm enough too.
Good morning! Oh, who are so happy as we?"
And away he went singing his chick-a-dee-dee.
    Chick-a-dee-dee, chick-a-dee-dee,
And merrily singing his chick-a-dee-dee.

—*F. C. Woodward.*

WAITING TO GROW.

LITTLE white snowdrop just waking up,
    Violet, daisy, and sweet buttercup,
Think of the flowers that are under the snow,
    Waiting to grow!

And think what a number of queer little seeds,
Of flowers and mosses, of ferns and of weeds,
Are under the leaves and under the snow,
    Waiting to grow!

Think of the roots getting ready to sprout,
Reaching their slender brown fingers about,
Under the ice and the leaves and the snow,
    Waiting to grow!

No seed is so small, or hidden so well,
That God cannot find it; and soon he will tell
His sun where to shine, and his rain where to go,
    Making it grow!
—*Selected.*

COME HERE, LITTLE ROBIN.

COME here, little Robin, and don't be afraid,
    I would not hurt even a feather;
Come here, little Robin, and pick up some bread,
    To feed you this very cold weather.

I don't mean to hurt you, you poor little thing!
    And Pussy cat is not behind me;
So hop about pretty, and put down your wing,
    And pick up the crumbs, and don't mind me.

Cold winter is come, but it will not last long,
    And summer we soon shall be greeting;
Then remember, sweet Robin, to sing me a song,
    In return for the breakfast you're eating.
—*Easy Poetry.*

WHAT THE SNOW-BIRDS SAID.

"Cheep, cheep," said some little snow-birds,
    As the snow came whirling down;
      "We haven't a nest,
      Or a place of rest,
    Save this oak-tree bending down."

"Cheep, cheep," said little Wee-Wing,
    The smallest bird of all;
      "I have never a care,
      In the winter air —
    God cares for great and small."

"Peep, peep," said her father, Gray-Breast,
    You're a thoughtless bird, my dear.
      We all must eat,
      And warm our feet,
    When snow and ice are here."

"Cheep, cheep," said little Wee-Wing,
    "You are wise and good, I know;
      But think of the fun
      For each little one,
    When we have ice and snow.

"Now I can see, from my perch on the tree,
    The merriest, merriest sight —
      Boys skating along
      On the ice so strong —
    Cheep, cheep, how merry and bright!"

"And I," said Brownie Snow-bird,
  "A sight that is prettier, far —
    Five dear little girls,
    With clustering curls,
  And eyes as bright as a star."

"And I," said his brother Bright-Eyes,
  "See a man of ice and snow;
    He wears a queer hat,
    His large nose is flat —
  The little boys made him, I know."

"I see some sleds," said Mother Brown,
  "All filled with girls and boys;
    They laugh and sing,
    Their voices ring,
  And I like the cheerful noise."

Then the snow-birds all said, "Cheep and chee,
  Hurrah for ice and snow;
    For the girls and boys,
    Who drop us crumbs,
  As away to their sport they go!

"Hurrah for the winter, clear and cold,
  When the dainty snowflakes fall!
    We will sit and sing,
    On our oaken swing,
  For God takes care of us all!"

—Selected.

OUR SIR ROBIN.

WHEN icicles shine so bright,
    Telling of cold weather,
Then we see Sir Robin bright,
    Rich in scarlet feather.
Sharp brown eyes, and sober suit,
Robin's voice is ever mute —
    Pretty winter Robin!

When the rosebuds are in bloom,
    Telling summer's near,
Then we hear the voice of Robin
    Singing loud and clear.
Of all wildwood birds, the best,
Robin of the red, red breast —
    Pretty winter robin!

— Selected.

THE CHRISTMAS SILENCE.

HUSHED are the pigeons cooing low,
    On dusty rafters of the loft;
    And mild-eyed oxen, breathing soft,
Sleep on the fragrant hay below.

Dim shadows in the corner hide;
    The glimmering lantern's rays are shed
    Where one young lamb just lifts his head,
Then huddles against his mother's side.

Strange silence tingles in the air;
   Through the half-open door a bar
   Of light from one low hanging star
Touches a baby's radiant hair —

No sound — the mother, kneeling, lays
   Her cheek against the little face.
   Oh, human love! Oh, heavenly grace!
'Tis yet in silence that she prays!

Ages of silence end to-night;
   Then to the long-expectant earth
   Glad angels come to greet His birth
In burst of music, love, and light!
— *Margaret Deland.*

MERRY CHRISTMAS.

IN the hush of early morning,
   When the red burns through the gray,
And the wintry world lies waiting
   For the glory of the day,
Then we hear a fitful rustling
   Just without upon the stair,
See two small white phantoms coming,
   Catch the gleam of sunny hair.

Are they Christmas fairies stealing
   Rows of little socks to fill?
Are they angels floating hither
   With their message of good-will?

What sweet spells are these elves weaving,
   As like larks they chirp and sing?
Are these palms of peace from heaven
   That these lovely spirits bring?

Rosy feet upon the threshold,
   Eager faces peeping through,
With the first red ray of sunshine,
   Chanting cherubs come in view;
Mistletoe and gleaming holly,
   Symbols of a blessed day,
In their chubby hands they carry,
   Streaming all along the way.

Well we know them, never weary
   Of this innocent surprise;
Waiting, watching, listening always,
   With full hearts and tender eyes,
While our little household angels,
   White and golden in the sun,
Greet us with the sweet old welcome, —
   "Merry Christmas, every one!"

—Selected.

HOLLY.

NOT one pretty flower would stay,
   When old Autumn nipped the grass;
For she had a cruel way,
   Though as red-cheeked as a lass.
   Winter had our Northland taken,
   Her white flags by wind outshaken.

What then was there bright enough
  For the merry Christmas Day?
"Good Dame Nature, be less rough,"
Said the folks, "leave storms, we pray;
    Bring some posies and be cheery,
    Lest she find the world too dreary."

"What are posies in the gleam
  Of my beautiful white frost?"
Said the old dame from her dream.
  "By the hedge all snow-embossed,
    Bloom itself the glad day carries,"
    And she held up holly berries.

How their scarlet brightness shone
  In the morning's airy tracks!
Nature is a wise old crone;
  She knows what a picture lacks.
    Winter lost its melancholy;
    Christmas laughed to see the holly.

Since that hour, now far away,
  When Time's tired wing was light,
In the path of Christmas Day
  Always shine the berries bright;
    And 'mid all its tender folly,
    Gleams the blush of Christmas holly.
                      — *Susan Hartley.*

SAID TULIP, "THAT IS SO."

ONE Christmas time some roots and bulbs,
    That lived far under ground,
Began to talk so softly that
    Above was heard no sound.
Said Hyacinth, " It seems a shame
    That we should have no share
In all the fun that's going on ;
    It really is not fair.
We hear the merry, jingling bells,
    As sleighs fly o'er the snow,
But cannot see a single thing."
    Said Tulip, " That is so."

Said Crocus, " I would like my dress
    Of shining gold to don."
Said Scilla, " O, I wish I could
    My bright blue gown put on."
" And much I long to join the dance,
    For none can rival me
In grace, the wind has oft declared,"
    Said fair Anemone.
" And would," Narcissus said, " I might
    My silver trumpet blow ;
'Twould glad, I'm sure, the Christmas green."
    Said Tulip, " That is so."

Then spoke the Snowdrop, " Cease to wish,
    For wishes are in vain ;
Here must we stay until we're called
    Above the ground again.

The blessing of a perfect rest
  At Christmas time is ours,
That we may gather strength to deck
  The earth, in spring, with flowers;
So sleep again, my sisters, dear,
  Till it is time to grow,
And all your dreams shall pleasant be."
  Said Tulip, "That is so."
                            — *Madge Elliot.*

WINTER APPLES.

WHAT cheer is there that is half so good,
  In the snowy waste of a winter night,
As a dancing fire of hickory wood,
  And an easy-chair in its mellow light,
    And a pearmain apple, ruddy and sleek,
    Or a jenetting with a freckled cheek?

A russet apple is fair to view,
  With a tanny tint like an autumn leaf,
The warmth of a ripen'd corn-field's hue,
  Or golden hint of a harvest sheaf;
    And the wholesome breath of the finished year
    Is held in a winecup's blooming sphere.

They bring you a thought of the orchard trees,
  In blossomy April and leafy June,
And the sleeepy droning of bumble-bees
  In the lazy light of the afternoon,
    And tangled clover and bobolinks,
    Tiger-lilies and garden pinks.

If you've somewhere left, with its gable wide,
  A farm-house set in an orchard old,
You'll see it all in the winter-tide,
  At sight of a pippin's green and gold,
    Or a pearmain apple, ruddy and sleek,
    Or a jenetting with a freckled cheek.

—Hattie Whitney — St. Nicholas.

DANCE OF THE MONTHS.

THE New Year comes in with shout and laughter,
  And see, twelve months are following after!
First January all in white,
And February short and bright;
See breezy March go tearing round;
But tearful April makes no sound.
May brings a pole with flowers crowned,
And June strews roses on the ground.
A pop! A bang! July comes in;
Says August, "What a dreadful din!"
September brings her golden sheaves;
October waves her pretty leaves,
While pale November waits to see
December bring the Christmas tree.
They join their hands to make a ring,
And as they dance they merrily sing,
" Twelve months we are, you see us here,
We make the circle of the year.
We dance and sing, and children hear,
We wish you all a glad New Year."

—Selected.

THE LITTLE PINE-TREE.

(From the German.)

ONCE a little Pine-tree,
  In the forest ways,
Sadly sighed and murmured,
  Through the summer days.
"I am clad in needles —
  Hateful things!" he cried;
"All the trees about me
  Laugh in scornful pride.
    Broad their leaves and fair to see;
    Worthless needles cover me.

"Ah, could I have chosen,
  Then, instead of these,
Shining leaves should crown me,
  Shaming all the trees.
Broad as theirs and brighter,
  Dazzling to behold;
All of gleaming silver —
  Aye, of burnished gold.
    Then the rest would weep and sigh;
    None would be so fine as I."

Slept the little Pine-tree
  When the night came down,
While the leaves he wished for
  Budded on his crown.
All the forest wondered
  At the dawn, to see

What a golden fortune
  Decked this little tree.
    Then he sang and laughed aloud;
    Glad was he and very proud.

Foolish little Pine-tree!
  At the close of day,
Thro' the gloomy twilight
  Came a thief that way.
Soon the treasure vanished;
  Sighed the Pine, "Alas!
Would that I had chosen
  Leaves of crystal glass."
    Long and bitterly he wept,
    But with night again he slept.

Gladly in the dawning,
  Did he wake to find
That the gentle fairies
  Had again been kind.
How his blazing crystals
  Lit the morning air!
Never had the forest
  Seen a sight so fair.
    Then a driving storm did pass;
    All his leaves were shattered glass.

Humbly said the Pine-tree,
  "I have learned 'tis best
Not to wish for fortunes
  Fairer than the rest.
Glad were I, and thankful,
  If I might be seen

Like the trees about me,
  Clad in tender green."
    Once again he slumbered, sad;
    Once again his wish he had.

Broad his leaves and fragrant,
  Rich were they and fine,
Till a goat at noon-day
  Halted there to dine.
Then her kids came skipping
  Round the fated tree;
All his leaves could scarcely
  Make a meal for three.
    Every tender bud was nipt,
    Every branch and twig was stripped

Then the wretched Pine-tree
  Cried in deep despair,
"Would I had my needles;
  They were green and fair.
Never would I change them,"
  Sighed the little tree;
"Just as nature gave them
  They were best for me."
    Then he slept, and waked, and found
    All his needles safe and sound.

— *Eudora S. Bumstead.*

PINE NEEDLE.

IF Mother Nature patches the leaves of trees and vines,
   I'm sure she does her darning with the needles of the pines,
They are so long and slender; and somewhere in full view,
She has her threads of cobweb, and a thimble made of dew.

—Selected.

THREE TREES.

THE pine-tree grew in the wood,
   Tapering, straight, and high;
Stately and proud it stood,
   Black-green against the sky.
Crowded so close, it sought the blue,
And ever upward it reached and grew.

The oak-tree stood in the field.
   Beneath it dozed the herds;
It gave to the mower a shield,
   It gave a home to the birds.
Sturdy and broad, it guarded the farms
With its brawny trunk and knotted arms.

The apple-tree grew by the wall,
   Ugly and crooked and black;
But it knew the gardener's call,
   And the children rode on its back.
It scattered its blossoms upon the air,
It covered the ground with fruitage fair.

"Now, hey," said the pine, "for the wood!
   Come live with the forest band.
Our comrades will do you good,
   And tall and straight you will stand."
And he swung his boughs to a witching sound,
And flung his cones like coins around.

"O-ho!" laughed the sturdy oak;
   "The life of the field for me.
I weather the lightning-stroke;
   My branches are broad and free.
Grow straight and slim in the wood if you will,
Give me the sun and the wind-swept hill."

And the apple-tree murmured low,
   "I am neither straight nor strong;
Crooked my back doth grow
   With bearing my burdens long."
And it dropped its fruit as it dropped a tear,
And reddened the ground with fragrant cheer.

And the Lord of the harvest heard,
   And he said: "I have use for all;
For the bough that shelters a bird,
   For the beam that pillars a hall;
And grow they tall, or grow they ill,
They grow but to wait their Master's will."

So a ship of the oak was sent
   Far over the ocean blue,
And the pine was the mast that bent
   As over the waves it flew,
And the ruddy fruit of the apple-tree
Was borne to a starving isle of the sea.

Now the farmer grows like the oak,
   And the townsman is proud and tall;
The city and field are full of folk —
   But the Lord has need of all.

—Selected.

THE BODY.

From the top of my head to my tiny toes,
I am built of bones as every one knows.

These are the framework so strong within;
Outside they are covered with flesh and skin.

The parts of my body are only three,
My head, my trunk, and my limbs as you see.

My head has a back, two sides, and a crown,
All covered with hair, yellow, black, red, or brown.

And just in front, in the foremost place,
You plainly can see my neat little face.

My face has a forehead, nose, mouth, and chin,
Two cheeks where the dimples slip out and in.

Two eyes to see you when you are near,
Two ears like seashells, to help me to hear.

My neck and shoulders so broad and strong,
Arm, forearm, wrist, hand, and fingers so long.

My trunk, and my thighs, legs, ankles, and knees,
On two feet I stand, or run, if I please.

My joints are to bend, when I run, jump, or walk;
I've a little red tongue to help me to talk.

These make up my body, and now I will tell
What we all must do to keep strong and well.

To be neat and clean we must take great care,
Have plenty of sunshine and breathe the fresh air.

Eat nourishing food to make good blood; and then
We shall all become strong women and men.
— *Selected.*

TWO AND ONE.

TWO ears and only one mouth have you;
  The reason, I think, is clear;
It teaches, my child, that it will not do
  To talk about all you hear.

Two eyes and only one mouth have you;
  The reason of this must be
That you should learn that it will not do
  To talk about all you see.

Two hands and only one mouth have you;
  And it is worth while repeating;
The two are for work that you must do,
  The one is enough for eating.
— *Selected.*

WHAT THE COAL SAYS.

I AM as black as black can be,
    But yet I shine.
My home was deep within the earth,
    In a dark mine.
Ages ago I was buried there,
    And yet I hold
The sunshine and the heat which warmed
    That world of old.
Though black and cold I seem to be,
    Yet I can glow.
Just put me on a blazing fire,
    Then you will know.
                     —*Selected.*

THE CANARY'S STORY.

I HAVE a little mistress,
    Her name is Kitty Blair;
She always used to give me
    The very best of care.
But now she has two Dollies
    She never thinks of me,
And I'm just as much neglected
    As a little bird can be.

When I sing my very sweetest,
    As I always try to do,
She covers up my cage, and says,
    "Oh, what a great ado!

I'm sure I shall be deafened!"
    Then she starts and runs away,
And I see no more of Kitty
    Through all the weary day.

My bath is always empty now,
    And I've very little seed;
When I've had a lump of sugar
    'Twould be hard to tell, indeed.
My cage is quite untidy,
    But Kitty heeds it not;
And I call her, oh! how vainly —
    For alas! I am forgot.

I've trilled my sweetest melodies;
    Alas! 'tis all in vain.
I'll fold my head beneath my wing
    And never more complain.
"My heart is broken, Kitty,
    But I'll forgive you, dear;
And I'm sure you will be sorry
    And will shed for me a tear."

When Kitty heard the mournful strain,
    Her heart was full of grief.
She left her Dollies then in haste,
    And ran to his relief.
She put fresh paper on the floor,
    And seed within the cup,
And water in the tiny bath,
    Then took poor Birdie up,

And gently stroked his yellow wings,
    And whispered words so low,

I think he must have understood,
  For this I surely know:
He opened wide his bright, black eye,
  Then on his perch he flew,
And poured such tide of melody
  As mortal never knew.

—E. V. S.

THE LITTLE KITTENS.

TWO little kittens, one stormy night,
  Began to quarrel and then to fight;
One had a mouse, the other had none,
And that was the way the quarrel begun.

"I'll have that mouse," said the bigger cat.
"You'll have that mouse? We'll see about that."
"I will have that mouse," said the elder son.
"You won't have that mouse!" said the little one.

I told you before 'twas a stormy night
When these two little kittens began to fight;
The old woman seized her sweeping broom,
And swept the two kittens right out of the room.

The ground was covered with frost and snow,
And the two little kittens had nowhere to go;
So they laid them down on the mat at the door,
While the angry old woman was sweeping the floor.

And then they crept in as quiet as mice,
All wet with snow, and as cold as ice;

For they found it was better, that stormy night,
To lie down and sleep than to quarrel and fight.
—*Selected.*

THEY DIDN'T THINK.

ONCE a trap was baited
   With a piece of cheese;
It tickled so a little mouse
   It almost made him sneeze;
An old rat said, "There's danger,
   Be careful where you go!"
"Nonsense!" said the other,
   "I don't think you know!"
So he walked in boldly —
   Nobody in sight;
First he took a nibble,
   Then he took a bite;
Close the trap together
   Snapped as quick as wink,
Catching mousey fast there,
   'Cause he didn't think.

Once a little turkey,
   Fond of her own way,
Wouldn't ask the old ones
   Where to go or stay;
She said, "I'm not a baby,
   Here I am half-grown;
Surely I am big enough
   To run about alone!"

Off she went, but somebody
   Hiding saw her pass;
Soon like snow her feathers
   Covered all the grass.
So she made a supper
   For a sly young mink,
'Cause she was so headstrong
   That she wouldn't think.

Once there was a robin
   Lived outside the door,
Who wanted to go inside
   And hop upon the floor.
"No, no," said the mother,
   "You must stay with me;
Little birds are safest
   Sitting in a tree."
"I don't care," said Robin,
   And gave his tail a fling,
"I don't think the old folks
   Know quite everything."
Down he flew, and Kitty seized him,
   Before he'd time to blink;
"Oh," he cried, "I'm sorry,
   But I didn't think."

Now, my little children,
   You who read this song,
Don't you see what trouble
   Comes of thinking wrong?
And can't you take a warning
   From their dreadful fate
Who began their thinking
   When it was too late?

Don't think there's always safety
    When no danger shows;
Don't suppose you know more
    Than anybody knows;
But when you're warned of ruin,
    Pause upon the brink,
And don't go under headlong,
    'Cause you didn't think.
                        — *Phœbe Cary.*

THE BEAUTIFUL ISLAND OF CEYLON.

OH, this beautiful island of Ceylon
    With the cocoanut-trees on the shore,
It is shaped like a pear with the peel on,
    And Kandy lies in at the core.

And Kandy is sweet (you ask Gertie)
    Even when it is spelt with a K,
And the people are cheerful and dirty,
    And dress in a comical way.

Here comes a particular dandy,
    With two ear-rings and half of a shirt;
He's considered the swell of all Kandy,
    And the rest of him's covered with dirt.

And here comes the belle of the city,
    With rings on her delicate toes,
And eyes that are painted and pretty,
    And a jewel that shakes in her nose.

And the dear little girls and their brothers;
   And the babies so jolly and fat,
Astride on the hips of their mothers
   And as black as a gentleman's hat.

And the queer little heaps of old women;
   And the shaven Buddhistical priests;
And the lake which the worshipers swim in;
   And the wagons with curious beasts.

The tongue they talk mostly is Tamul,
   Which sounds you can hardly tell how;
It is half like the scream of a camel,
   And half like the grunt of a sow.
— Phillips Brooks.

THE FERRY FOR SHADOWTOWN.

Sway to and fro in the twilight gray;
   This is the ferry for Shadowtown;
It always sails at the end of the day,
   Just as the darkness closes down.

Rest, little head, on my shoulder so;
   A sleepy kiss is the only fare;
Drifting away from the world we go,
   Baby and I in the rocking-chair.

See, where the fire-logs glow and spark,
   Glitter the lights of the shadowland;
The raining drops on the window, — hark!
   Are ripples lapping upon its strand.

There, where the mirror is glancing dim,
   A lake lies shimmering, cool and still;
Blossoms are waving above its brim,
   Those over there on the window-sill.

Rock slow, more slow in the dusky light,
   Silently lower the anchor down.
Dear little passenger, say " Good-night ! "
   We've reached the harbor for Shadowtown!
                        —*Motherhood.*

THE STARS' BALL.

OH! the stars, one and all,
   They had a great ball
     One night, way up in the sky;
They invited the Earth
To join in their mirth,
     But it feared to go up so high.

No fiddler had they
Their music to play,
     And the stars were afraid 'twould fail;
But the man in the moon
He whistled a tune,
     And the comet kept time with his tail.

They danced, and they danced,
And they pranced, and they pranced,
     Till the Moon said 'twas all he desired;
For his lips were so sore
He could whistle no more,
     And the comet began to get tired.

So they faded away
In the dim light of day,
   The moon and the stars from the ball.
But sad to relate,
Next night they were late,
   And came near not shining at all.
                  —*Ladies' Home Journal.*

OUR FLAG.

FLAG of our country brave,
   Red, white, and blue,
We love to watch thee wave;
   Our love is true.
Oh! let us loudly sing!
Loudly let our praises ring,
Praise to this noble thing,
   Red, white, and blue.

Red is the blood that rolls;
   Blue is the sky;
White are the heroes' souls,
   For thee that die.
Oh! let us loudly sing!
Loudly let our praises ring,
Praise that this holy thing
   Still waves on high.

Broad is our native land,—
   Land of the free,
'Mong all the nations grand,
   Foremost to be.

Oh! let us loudly sing!
Thanks unto our God and King,
Thanks for this noble thing,
   Father, to Thee!

—*Selected.*

HURRAH FOR THE FLAG.

THERE are many flags in many lands,
   There are flags of every hue,
But there is no flag, however grand,
   Like our own " Red, White, and Blue."

I know where the prettiest colors are,
   And I'm sure if I only knew
How to get them here I could make a flag
   Of glorious " Red, White, and Blue."

I would cut a piece from an evening sky,
   Where the stars were shining through,
And use it just as it was on high,
   For my stars and field of blue.

Then I'd want a part of a fleecy cloud,
   And some red from a rainbow bright;
And put them together side by side,
   For my stripes of red and white.

We shall always love the " Stars and Stripes,"
   And we mean to be ever true
To this land of ours and the dear old flag,
   The Red, the White, and the Blue.

Then hurrah for the flag ! our country's flag,
   Its stripes and white stars too;
There is no flag in any land,
   Like our own " Red, White, and Blue !"
—Selected.

SWEET AND LOW.

SWEET and low, sweet and low,
   Wind of the western sea;
Low, low, breathe and blow,
   Wind of the western sea!
Over the rolling waters go,
Come from the dying moon, and blow,
   Blow him again to me;
While my little one, while my pretty one, sleeps.

Sleep and rest, sleep and rest,
   Father will come to thee soon;
Rest, rest, on mother's breast,
   Father will come to thee soon;
Father will come to his babe in the nest,
Silver sails all out of the west,
   Under the silver moon;
Sleep, my little one, sleep, my pretty one, sleep.
—Tennyson.

DUTCH LULLABY.

WYNKEN, Blynken, and Nod one night
   Sailed off in a wooden shoe,—
Sailed on a river of misty light
   Into a sea of dew.
"Where are you going, and what do you wish?
   The old moon asked the three.
"We have come to fish for the herring-fish
   That live in this beautiful sea;
   Nets of silver and gold have we,"
       Said Wynken,
       Blynken,
       And Nod.

The old moon laughed and sung a song,
   As they rocked in the wooden shoe;
And the wind that sped them all night long,
   Ruffled the waves of dew;
The little stars were the herring-fish
   That lived in the beautiful sea.
"Now cast your nets wherever you wish,
   But never afeard are we!"
   So cried the stars to the fishermen three,—
       Wynken,
       Blynken,
       And Nod.

All night long their nets they threw
   For the fish in the twinkling foam,
Then down from the sky came the wooden shoe,
   Bringing the fishermen home;

'Twas all so pretty a sail, it seemed
  As if it could not be ;
And some folk thought 'twas a dream they'd dreamed,
  Of sailing that beautiful sea ;
But I shall name you the fishermen three,—
    Wynken,
    Blynken,
    And Nod.

Wynken and Blynken are two little eyes,
  And Nod is a little head,
And the wooden shoe that sailed the skies
  Is a wee one's trundle-bed ;
So shut your eyes while mother sings
  Of wonderful sights that be,
And you shall see the beautiful things
  As you rock on the misty sea
Where the old shoe rocked the fishermen three,—
    Wynken,
    Blynken,
    And Nod.
    —*Eugene Field—A Little Book of Western Verse.*

GOOD-NIGHT.

GOOD-NIGHT, pretty Sun, good-night!
  I've watched your purple and golden light
  While you are sinking away ;
And some one has just been telling me
You're making o'er the shining sea
  Another beautiful day ;
That just at the time I am going to sleep,

The children there are taking a peep
  At your face, — beginning to say,
"Good-morning!" just when I say "good-night!"
Now, beautiful Sun, if they've told me right,
  I wish you'd say good-morning for me
    To all the little ones over the sea.

— *Sydney Dayre.*

NOW THE DAY IS OVER.

NOW the day is over,
  Night is drawing nigh,
Shadows of the evening
  Steal across the sky.

Through the long night-watches,
  May Thine angels spread
Their white wings above us;
  Watching round each bed.

When the morning wakens
  Then may I arise
Pure, and fresh, and sinless,
  In Thy holy eyes.

— *Sabine Baring-Gould.*

The Fundamentals in Education.

Standard and Popular Text-books in Reading, Spelling, Writing, Language, and Number; also in Drawing and Music.

The Normal Course in Reading. By EMMA J. TODD, formerly Training Teacher in the Public Schools of Aurora, Ill., and W. B. POWELL, A.M., Superintendent of City Schools, Washington, D.C.

This series includes a Primer, New First Reader, Second Reader, Third Reader, Fourth Reader, and Fifth Reader, besides Alternate First, Second, and Third Readers.

The Normal Course in Spelling. For Public and Private Schools. By LARKIN DUNTON, LL.D., Head Master of the Boston Normal School, and C. GOODWIN CLARK, A.M., late Master of the Gaston School.

This course includes a Primary Book, Advanced Book, and Complete Course, besides Spelling Blanks.

The Normal Review System of Writing. By D. H. FARLEY, Professor of Penmanship in the State Normal School of New Jersey, at Trenton, and W. B. GUNNISON, Principal of Public School No. 19, Brooklyn, N.Y., Ex-President of the New York State Teachers' Association.

This system includes both slanting and vertical copies, with a Manual of Vertical Writing.

The Normal Course in English. By Prof. ALFRED H. WELSH and J. M. GREENWOOD, Superintendent of Schools, Kansas City, Mo.

This course includes "The Elements of Language and Grammar," and "Studies in English Grammar."

The Normal Course in Number. By JOHN W. COOK, President of Illinois State Normal University, and Miss N. CROPSEY, Assistant Superintendent of City Schools, Indianapolis, Ind.

This course includes an Elementary Arithmetic and the New Advanced Arithmetic.

The Normal Course in Drawing. By Prof. H. W. SHAYLOR, Director of Drawing and Penmanship in the Public Schools of Portland, Me.

This course includes nine numbers, besides a blank Drawing-Book and a Handbook for Teachers.

The Normal Music Course. By JOHN W. TUFTS and H. E. HOLT. A complete Series of Music Readers and Charts, for every grade of School and Class Instruction in Vocal Music.

SILVER, BURDETT & COMPANY, Publishers.

Boston.   New York.   Philadelphia.   Chicago.

CPSIA information can be obtained at www.ICGtesting.com
Printed in the USA
LVOW052156251012

304457LV00014B/71/P